The Great Eight
MANAGEMENT STRATEGIES for the
Reading and Writing Classroom

PAM ALLYN • JAIME MARGOLIES • KAREN McNALLY

NEW YORK • TORONTO • LONDON • AUCKLAND • SYDNEY
MEXICO CITY • NEW DELHI • HONG KONG • BUENOS AIRES

Dedication

To the teachers and children with whom we work and coach, and whose joyful engagement with reading and writing is reflected here in every page.

Acknowledgments

With our appreciation to our great team at Scholastic: luminous Lois Bridges, dedicated Danny Miller, gifted Gloria Pipkin, magical Maria Lilja, extraordinary Eileen Hillebrand. You each touch these pages with your bountiful knowledge and remarkable insights. We thank our agent Lisa DiMona, who shepherds our books so carefully from beginning to end. We are—as always— grateful beyond measure to our colleagues at LitLife, who inspire us every day with their innovative ideas and graceful sharings. Our gratitude also goes to Jen Estrada and Dorothy Lee, who added loving care to this book process. We honor our families: Jaime's Aaron and Ellie; Karen's Chris, Jack, Kiera, and Drew; Pam's Jim, Katie, and Charlotte, for their joyous support and for their own wisdom as to what really works in classrooms! We're also indebted to the extraordinary teachers whose work informs these pages and delights the lives of children: Kerri Bernard, Nadia Cortina, Ruth Ann Cosgrove, Carol-Ann Cristella, Allison DeLesia, Kathy Dragonetti, Danielle Esposito, Keri Fischer, Janet Knight, Jeanette Magnani, Felicia Maldari, Erin McCall, Juliett Roskell, Christina Schilli, Shannon Smith, Rachel Tortorella, and all our partner schools, which demonstrate excellence every day. Special thanks go to Port Chester Public Schools, Blindbrook Public Schools, and the Pave Charter Academy for their enthusiasm and willingness to share the beauty of their classrooms and children with us.

Cover and interior design by Maria Lilja
Photos by LitLife Archives (interior), Maria Lilja (cover)
Acquiring Editor: Lois Bridges
Production Editor: Gloria Pipkin
Copy Editor: Danny Miller

ISBN-13: 978-0-545-17353-7
ISBN-10: 0-545-17353-1
Copyright © 2010 by LitLife Publishing LLC

Contents

The Great Eight: The Perfect Recipe

Collectively, my colleagues and I spend thousands of hours each year in classrooms. On behalf of our organization, LitLife, we coach teachers on best-practice reading and writing instruction. We understand you want to bring instruction that matters to students and that creates extraordinary outcomes. Given the constraints of classroom life and the sheer intensity of time, not to mention the tender, complex lives that are under your care over the course of each school year, this is no small task, and guidance helps.

We know you want the practical nuts-and-bolts information and resources that will guarantee successful outcomes in the teaching of reading and writing. We recognize that, as with cooking, a good recipe for classroom success is clear, with a finite number of easy-to-use ingredients that will be enjoyed by all.

We aim to provide you with a tried-and-true recipe for creating the ideal reading and writing classroom. The "Great Eight" in the title of this book refers to our most essential management ingredients to support your best year ever.

When I (Pam) was first married, I began to learn how to cook. I remembered that long ago my grandmother had said to me that behind every great cook was a great recipe. I had always thought she was a terrific cook herself. It was my mother, years later, who told me that my grandmother "Gigi" had really only learned a few good recipes, which she prepared for her adoring family every single Sunday of her married life. This was in addition to her teaching and counseling career. Her meals were full of love and care, and, in retrospect, I realize they were precise: a highly structured approach to a loving presentation. And the more I think about it, the more I see what a perfect metaphor that is for our own teaching and the way we want to be with our students all year long. My colleagues Jaime Margolies and Karen McNally have made it their lifework to help teachers build classrooms that are highly structured yet deeply personal. This is no easy feat. Yet somehow, they do it, over and over and over. Which shows me that it can be done— with sensible, logical guidance we can all create extraordinary classrooms in which all children learn to read and write.

Students need structure. A recipe is a structure. When I started to learn how to cook soup, I went to my grandmother's recipe. And I practiced it. I studied every aspect of it, and I deliberated over all the ingredients. I practiced the small details, like how to cut an onion. I went to the butcher and landed the most important big detail: the perfect chicken.

On that fateful night I tried the recipe, I was wearing my wedding ring, as always. But at the end of the night, drenched in chicken fat (sorry, vegetarian readers!) and weeping from chopped onions, I was no longer wearing my ring. Not because of anything in the marriage (no worries, romantic readers!), but because somehow, somewhere in the middle of that soup-making frenzy, my ring, slick with chicken fat, had slipped off my finger and dropped, I thought, into that pot of soup.

When my husband came home, I was weeping true tears of despair... for the soup, for my utter lack of confidence in my cooking, and for my lost ring. Good husband that he is, he sat there and tenderly, carefully, and oh-so-slowly ate that entire pot of soup. We never found the ring, though he looked in every spoonful. It was a mystery. But within the savory ingredients of that soup were my grandmother, her sheer determination and love for passion and structure; my husband, his love for me and his ineffable, inexhaustible patience for every new idea I have; my mother, who outed my grandmother as a cook with four or five good recipes and not much more, but with an understanding that those five were all that really counted; and myself, newly married, full of love and hope and passion, trying to follow the good recipe.

My brilliant colleagues Jaime Margolies and Karen McNally are the geniuses of this book—the teaching chefs of all chefs. *The Great Eight: Management Strategies for the Reading and Writing Classroom* is our collective recipe to create the kinds of classrooms I dream about for all schools in this country and in the world. We embrace great recipes: At home we ask our mothers, our grandmothers, our fathers, our husbands for the perfect recipe to give our families just what they need. So why should we ever be afraid to ask for the perfect recipe for our classrooms? This recipe is informed by our years on the ground in classrooms across this country. Our team at LitLife works side by side with teachers and students to improve reading and writing outcomes. We identify the crucial ingredients that can't be missed. Each of the "Great Eight" components reflects one essential ingredient to help you create your own harmonious, learning-rich classroom.

Our team has written a series of books titled The Complete Year in Reading and Writing. They are a program of units of study linking reading and writing instruction, and they are based on a groundbreaking concept known as the Complete 4. We developed the Complete 4 to help teachers build a yearlong program for teaching both reading and writing that feels far more connected and integrated than anything that has come before it. Throughout this book we will highlight the Complete 4 when applicable.

And the wedding ring? Maybe that was my secret ingredient! I was full of love for my husband and for our life to come, for the family we would create, and the home we would build. What is your secret ingredient for a successful classroom? Your own joy and love for teaching? Your feelings about the children? Your memories of your own great teachers or your own great family? All of these elements become part of your own special recipe for success. You can follow a recipe and be yourself at the same time. That is what this book is about.

This book, created with love and care, is a guaranteed recipe for success. Its eight magical ingredients will allow you to teach reading and writing more powerfully than ever before. Follow this recipe, but find your own secret ingredients. Behind every great teacher, my grandmother would have said, is a perfect recipe. We hope *The Great Eight* will be yours.

Pam Allyn   Jaime Margolies   Karen McNally

Setting Up Wisely: Walls, Floors, and More

When we first enter our classrooms our hearts surge with excitement. The spacc is a palette upon which we can create our hopes and dreams for our children. And yet the reality of our spaces may prevent us from imagining the perfect environment. The walls may be nicked and chipped, the floors cold and grey. We could easily get discouraged. Yet we know how much environment matters. It matters to us every day: Surroundings that feel peaceful and optimistic, inspiring and energizing help us even as adults to do our best work.

Plan your physical space wisely to create a successful classroom environment.

And so, when we open our doors to new students each year, we have spent a lot of time thinking about where things go and how things look. Every detail matters. The wise placement of our furniture will allow easy access for movement around the room. The walls will reflect what we value: What we choose to put there and what the students will put there as the year unfolds tells the story of our learning. We will select rugs to create meeting areas for our community learning. We will put our reading and writing tools in places for easy access. All of these careful plans set the tone for our new learning environment, our learning home for the next ten months.

In many ways, creating a thoughtful physical and emotional classroom environment is like cooking your favorite soup. Everyone's soup tastes a little different, but the most delicious ones have been carefully assembled, designed to blend together the ingredients while bringing out the flavors of each. We set up our rooms with care because they will be our containers for learning, the perfect pot for our wonderful teaching soup. This is the first Great Eight Strategy: Setting Up Wisely.

Organized Classroom Space

An organized, clutter-free space is critical to creating a classroom that inspires contemplation and learning rather than distraction. Charts must be useful and placed strategically around the room. Student work should be clearly labeled and organized. Teacher space should also be free of clutter and in order. Take a close look at the classroom in the photo above. It is inviting because it is well organized. Let's journey inside.

Wall Space

The walls in our classrooms tell the story of our students' learning. Work that is displayed should be highly relevant to recent teaching. Fill your wall space with both student work and anchor charts that match current instruction. The walls should be useful resources for our students: reminders of their responsibilities, support for the skills they're developing, and a celebration of the work they have done.

Rules and Responsibilities

Some of our wall space is reserved for our class rules and responsibilities, written together with the students. The tone is set for our learners when we write these rules in the positive instead of the negative. For example, instead of saying, "Do not hit others," we can say "We will be safe with our bodies." Instead of saying, "Don't be mean to other students," we say, "We will treat one another kindly, with respect." Some other important rules that will set the tone for our primary students include sharing materials, using time well during independent practice, always allowing others to join in, and listening to one another and the teacher.

Some wall space is reserved for class rules and responsibilities, written in a positive tone by students and teacher working together.

Word Walls

An important feature of our wall space in primary classrooms is the word wall. This space is a helpful resource for students when writing; it's another way to support them when accessing words. Here are five tips to support the use of word walls in your classroom.

- Make sure words are large enough for all students to see from across the room. If the print is too small, students will be unable to read the words from their writing spots.
- Design word walls that are interactive, a space where students can take copies of words and bring them to and from their writing spots.
- Start small. At the beginning of the year, the word wall should be blank or filled just with names of students in the class. The word wall evolves over time, with no more than five words added each week.

- Start with smaller common sight words and continue from there. It is important that students can read the words on the word wall.
- Discuss each word that you enter on the wall. Words that go on the word wall need to be reviewed with the whole class for several days before they are added to the wall.

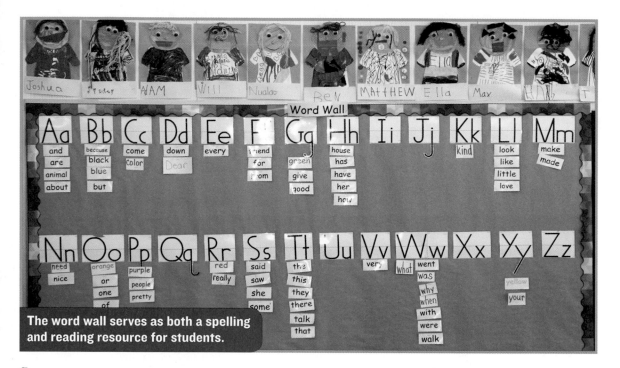

The word wall serves as both a spelling and reading resource for students.

Classroom charts are written with students and include picture support for our youngest learners.

Anchor Charts

The charts that surround us directly reflect our teaching. They are written in large print with pictures to support our youngest learners and are created during teaching time. At the beginning of the year, our charts focus on the routines and structures of reading and writing workshops. They explicitly state what is expected of our students in simple language that they can follow.

Over time, our charts will change; old charts will be replaced with new charts to support the newest reading and writing work. You can walk into a classroom and know by the surrounding charts the lessons we are teaching. For example, during a set of lessons in nonfiction reading and writing, you will find charts that support this work. You may see a chart on the features or structures of nonfiction books.

Student Work

One of the best ways to celebrate student work is to display it prominently. This work should be recent and will therefore change over time (approximately every four to six weeks). In kindergarten and first grade, you may see authentic work with developmental spelling that has not been "edited" by the teachers. By second grade, the work that hangs on the walls outside the classroom should reflect conventional spellings, but inside the classroom, if you would like to celebrate your students' step-by-step achievements, feel free to hang all their works in progress.

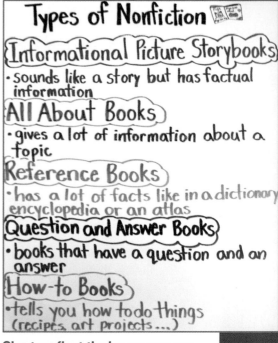

Charts reflect the lessons we are teaching. During sets of lessons in nonfiction reading and writing, we display charts supporting this work.

Honor and celebrate a student's attempt at spelling words independently. Do not require that all writing published within the classroom reflect conventional spelling. However, student writing that will be read by other students should be written in conventional spelling. For kindergartners and first graders, we word-process their writing using conventional spelling. The conventionally written version can be taped on the back of a facing page instead of directly over their writing so you can see both. This way, if it is featured in the hall, other students can read it easily. In second grade, students may rewrite a piece that has been edited by the teacher if the piece is not very long. If you are preparing for a writing celebration and want the spelling to be conventional, consider inviting parents or older students to help you type in preparation for a public display.

Classroom schedule

Schedules for our youngest learners include a picture next to the words to make sure students can access the information.

Classroom Schedule

Create daily schedules to manage and organize learning time throughout the day. This schedule is consistent and predictable for our students. The routine helps our students feel secure about the school day. Here are some options for sharing the classroom schedule with students.

- Write daily schedules on index cards and place them in pocket charts.

- Record schedules on magnetic strips and organize them on magnetic boards.

- Write schedules on index cards and use fabric hook-and-loop fasteners to post them in the classroom.

- List the daily schedule on chart paper and keep it at the front of the classroom for easy viewing.

Our primary students enthusiastically examine the day's schedule first thing each morning. If there is a change in the regular routine, they are the first to point it out! Schedules for our youngest learners include a picture next to the words to enable all students to access the information.

Book Signout and Center Chart

Some of the charts hanging on our walls can be interactive in nature, allowing students to use them for daily routines and activities. To this end, place a chart with library pockets and index cards low on the wall within easy reach of little ones who sign out their books each night and check off the books when they return them the next day. Another interactive chart

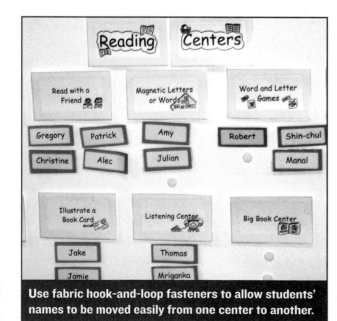

Use fabric hook-and-loop fasteners to allow students' names to be moved easily from one center to another.

Place library pockets and index cards low on the wall within easy reach.

for kindergarten and first grade is the center chart for students working in reading or play centers. If you make the chart with fabric hook-and-loop fasteners, students' names can easily be moved around from one center to another. Foam board is a great resource that works well for both charts.

Small-Group and Individual Schedules

Each day, display the names of the students who will be working in small instructional groups and conferences during reading and writing time. This way, students come in the morning to see their name listed for either a small group or a conference. Both you and your students will be more prepared for this essential instructional time together if names are posted before the students' arrival. You will find more information about small-group and individual instruction in Management Strategies #6 and #7.

Mailboxes

One way to save space is to use the back of your door for mailboxes. Hanging shoe-storage bags are very useful for this purpose. This way it is easy to put letters, notes, and homework into the bags, and student can collect these items when they pack up at the end of the school day. The Web sites Lakeshore (www.lakeshorelearning.com) and Really Good Stuff (www.reallygoodstuff.com) sell premade student mailboxes with narrow slots for each student— another way to organize notes and mail going home.

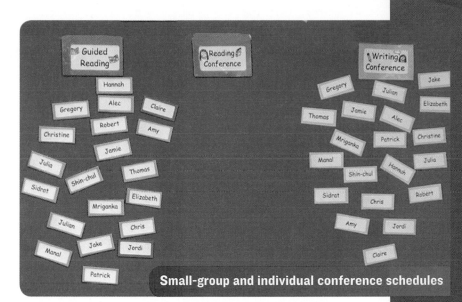

Small-group and individual conference schedules

Both you and your students will be more prepared for small-group work and conferences if names are posted before students' arrival.

Shoe bags mounted on the back of your door make useful mailboxes.

Floor Space

Just as we thoughtfully organize our wall space, we want to be equally as thoughtful about our floor space. Our rooms are set up in ways that make it very easy for students to move through the space and know where to go. The placement of our furniture and rugs greatly affects this flow.

Rug Area

In our classrooms, we have a central meeting area where all of our students can sit together for whole-group instruction. This meeting area is created with a rug or rug tiles. Using tape with the name of each student, we sometimes label rugs with a spot for each student to sit. Some rugs have colored or alphabet boxes to designate where students may sit. For the most efficient use of space, try to locate your rug and meeting area along a wall. You may need to try a few different spots before deciding the best place for the large rug.

For the most efficient use of space, try to locate your rug and meeting area along a wall.

Furniture

Where we place the furniture in our room dictates how students move through it. In a large classroom, it is easy to find a spot for furniture; a small classroom makes furniture placement a greater challenge. To set up for small spaces:

- Move your teacher desk against a wall to leave more space for other things, or get rid of the desk altogether.

- Arrange tables so they all face the same direction. This makes movement through the classroom easier and leaves more space for other furniture.

- Line your rug area with low bookshelves that hold your classroom library. This way your meeting area will serve as both your classroom library and a place for whole-group instruction.

- Make an aisle where students will line up to get in and out of the classroom with ease.

Place all tables facing the same way.

Make an aisle where students will line up.

Helpful Tip

Label student chairs: We often change where our students are sitting throughout the year so they have an opportunity to work with all of their classmates. One way to make this change easy is to label the backs of students' chairs instead of desks or tables. This means when students have a new working spot, they have to move only their chairs.

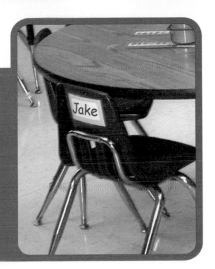

Organized Work Space

We organize our teacher and student work spaces as well as our floor and wall space. This sends the message that organization and respect for materials are important. You are the students' role model, so your space should reflect your own thoughtful learning and organized use of your learning tools.

Teacher Space

Teacher space is our sacred area to keep our materials and plans tidy and organized. The less clutter the better. Many classrooms offer only a small table, back counter, or bookshelf for the teacher's personal use. Here are the tools to have handy in this space.

Plan Book

Plan books can be found at teacher supply stores or can be created on the computer. When you create your planner on the computer, it is useful to list the components of your schedule each day to minimize the time needed to write plans. This way, it says *read-aloud* or *writing* every day and all you have to fill in is the specific lesson. Page 17 shows a sample computer-generated schedule.

Reserved Read-Alouds

Keep a bookshelf for instructional read-alouds. These books are organized by unit of study or topic for easy access and are considered a "reserved" area in the classroom. After reading aloud a book to students, add it to the read-aloud shelf for student access during partner or independent reading time. These books are given a special designation with a sticker on the inside cover, so students know to return them to the reserved area of the classroom when the time comes.

A basket that features favorite read-alouds allows easy access for students to choose books during partner or independent reading time.

Professional Books

Keep your professional books easily accessible, to support you when planning and thinking about your reading and writing work for students. See recommended reading on page 144.

Weekly Schedule

	Monday	Tuesday	Wednesday	Thursday	Friday
8:30–8:40	Arrival Unpack	Arrival Unpack	Arrival Unpack	Arrival Unpack	Arrival Unpack
8:40–9:00	Morning Meeting Read-Aloud Title:	Morning Meeting Read-Aloud Title:	Morning Meeting Read-Aloud Title:	Morning Meeting Read-Aloud Title:	Morning Meeting Read-Aloud Title:
9:00–9:15	Partner Reading	Partner Reading	Partner Reading	Partner Reading	Partner Reading
9:15–9:55	Reading Workshop Lesson:	Reading Workshop Lesson:	Reading Workshop Lesson:	Reading Workshop Lesson:	Reading Workshop Lesson:
9:55–10:10	Shared Reading	Shared Reading	Shared Reading	Shared Reading	Shared Reading
10:10–10:20	Snack	Snack	Snack	Snack	Snack
10:20–11:00	Writing Workshop Lesson:	Writing Workshop Lesson:	Writing Workshop Lesson:	Writing Workshop Lesson:	Writing Workshop Lesson:
11:00–11:15	Word Work Lesson:	Word Work Lesson:	Word Work Lesson:	Word Work Lesson:	Word Work Lesson:
11:15–12:15	Lunch/Recess	Lunch/Recess	Lunch/Recess	Lunch/Recess	Lunch/Recess
12:15–1:00	Math Lesson:	Math Lesson:	Math Lesson:	Math Lesson:	Math Lesson:
1:00–1:30	Centers OR Choice Time	Centers OR Choice Time	Centers OR Choice Time	Centers OR Choice Time	Centers OR Choice Time
1:30–2:15	Art	Gym	Library	Gym	Music
2:15–2:45	Science OR Social Studies	Science OR Social Studies	Science OR Social Studies	Science OR Social Studies	Science OR Social Studies
2:45–3:00	Goodbye Meeting Read-Aloud Title:	Goodbye Meeting Read-Aloud Title:	Goodbye Meeting Read-Aloud Title:	Goodbye Meeting Read-Aloud Title:	Goodbye Meeting Read-Aloud Title:
3:00–3:10	Pack Up Dismiss	Pack Up Dismiss	Pack Up Dismiss	Pack Up Dismiss	Pack Up Dismiss

Whole-Class Workspace

Your workspaces in the classroom should be equipped with everything you need for teaching, right at your fingertips. We can easily move students from whole-class to small-group and independent work if the necessary materials are ready to go!

The whole-class workspace, where you conduct meetings and lessons, includes the following:

- easel with chart paper and big book stand or an interactive whiteboard
- read-aloud ready for the day's instruction
- markers
- sticky notes
- bell (e.g., dinner bell, table-top bell, chime bell)
- timer

Whole-class workspace

Easel with chart paper and big book stand or an interactive whiteboard

Read-aloud ready for the day's instruction

Markers, sticky notes, bell, and timer

Your small-group workspace, where you conduct small-group reading and writing lessons, will include the following:

- books for small-group instruction (guided reading books)
- binder with plans for the small group
- pencils
- wipe-off boards and wipe-off markers
- magnetic boards (or old cookie sheets)
- magnetic letters
- sticky notes
- erasers for wipe-off boards
- laptops, if your students are reading online

Small-group workspace

Keeping student papers organized is a must. Students can be easily taught how to organize their papers into specific baskets. Label baskets or trays "Notes for Teacher" (from parents), "Homework," and "In Box." Teach students the purpose for each basket and the appropriate time each day to file their papers.

Top Five Tips for Setting Up Wisely to Create a Positive Tone

The tone we set in our classrooms has a direct impact on student performance. Our rooms should feel calm and welcoming, a place where students can focus and engage in their learning.

1 Find ways to reduce noise.

One major way to reduce the noise level in your classroom is by putting tennis balls on the bottom of chair legs. This will quiet transitions as students move around the classroom from whole groups to small groups and then back to whole groups again.

2 Use music to calm and signal transitions.

Keep students calm during both independent time and transition time by playing music. Play a song that signifies moving from one place in the room to another, always using the same song so it signals the movement. Classical music is an effective way to keep students relaxed and focused during independent reading and writing time.

3 Make lighting conducive to calm learning.

Use table lamps and standing lamps to create cozy environments; minimize the use of harsh fluorescent lighting. Shop for inexpensive lamps at garage sales and discount stores.

4 Cover clutter artfully.

Use swaths of fabric in warm colors to drape over the front of open shelves and cabinets. The resulting effect is similar to curtains and beautifully hides the distracting clutter behind it!

5 Use color to focus and invigorate.

The way we use colors in our classroom can greatly affect the mood of our space. Warm colors have been proven to make children feel calm and comfortable. Often, classroom rugs are designed with primary colors that make the room feel bold; we balance this with neutral colors on the walls and bulletin board spaces. The lasting effect is a calm, soothing learning environment. A good rule of thumb is to try to use colors that are found in nature rather than colors designed by a marketing team. Soft purples, gentle blues, and sea-foam greens all contribute to a peaceful environment. Use a splash of red or orange on one wall or bulletin board to make things cheery, or drape with a dynamic fabric, but do not overload your room with hard, strong colors.

You Asked, We Answered

Q How can I figure out the best way to set up my room with the furniture that was given to me?

A Try different places for your furniture and rugs. Ask your colleagues to come in, have a look, and suggest different options you might try. It is always easier when you have a second eye to look at the space. Make the room easy to move through and functional for all students, with places for whole-class, small-group, and independent work to occur. The WSW (whole, small, whole) model of instruction is supported by room arrangements that make those transitions easy.

Q I have a very small space and a lot of furniture. Is there something I can get rid of to make more space?

A It is hard to let go of furniture, but if we have a small space it may be necessary. Many teachers in small classrooms decide to get rid of their desk, which frees up considerable space. Teachers without desks often keep their supplies on a rolling cart or a back countertop. You may also be able to get rid of an extra table not used for student seating. Another space-saving tip: Avoid horseshoe-shaped tables as they take up a huge amount of space. Instead, meet with small groups at a round table or even on the rug.

Q How can I stay on top of classroom setup?

A There are many important aspects of setting up your classroom. We have created a Classroom Environment Checklist that will help you prepare your classroom for your students. The guidelines in Resource 1.1 (page 112) will support you in thinking about the different areas of your classroom and the best ways to get ready.

Organized classroom materials support learning.

Creating the Perfect Space

Our classrooms should encourage learning during quiet, independent moments, as well as during big whole-class teaching moments, giving our students plentiful opportunities to reach their full learning potential. Take time to manage your space and reflect upon it every day. Each and every day, sing a "clean-up" song or put on music so you and your students can clean up your own spaces. Reduction of clutter is a surefire way to ease your mind and the minds of your learners. And in this way you can see more clearly how the classroom functions and whether or not your "flow" is working well. Ask yourself:

- Is it easy for me and my students to move around in here?
- Do my students know where everything is?
- Is the space soothing for us all? Is it inspirational for independent work?
- Are spaces clearly identified as to their purpose and role in the room?

This is important work, although its value is often underestimated. Teachers will say to us: "I'm too busy to clean up!" Don't ever feel this is an unimportant aspect of your work. It is good, hard physical work that can make all the difference for you and for your students. In the next section we address the management and organization of reading and writing materials. We provide concrete systems and visual supports that will bring order and functionality to your classroom.

A small classroom can still provide a cozy space for readers and places for all materials.

Organizing Materials: Classroom Libraries and Writing Centers

Our students come into our classrooms full of creative energy. To tap into that creativity, we must make it easy and natural for them to share their ideas and invent new ones. Students will be most successful when we create opportunities for them to work in organized environments. We want our students to understand that their classroom is their home away from home and that we must all work together to take care of it—returning items to their rightful places and treating the materials with care. The second Great Eight strategy is to organize materials with flair, intention, and purpose.

The Classroom Library

The classroom library is the center of a classroom, inspiring and exciting students, and a place where they feel cozy and comfortable. Books are organized and easily accessible. In the library, there is a place for everything, and everything has a place. Our libraries should be chock-full of rich literature and extremely well organized so students know where to get books based on genre, interest, or level.

A welcoming, well-organized classroom library

Organizing books in wooden boxes

Choosing Books

Fill your library with books that will interest your students and books that are appropriate to their grade level. In kindergarten, our libraries house picture books in different genres (fiction, nonfiction, and poetry), as well as leveled books. In first grade, we begin to add early chapter books from series, such as Henry and Mudge by Cynthia Rylant, Nate the Great by Marjorie Weinman Sharmat, and Little Bear by Else Holmelund Minarik. As we move into second grade, we continue to feature many picture books, but we begin to add even more early chapter book series, such as Magic Tree House by Mary Pope Osborne and Cam Jansen by David A. Adler.

Read-Alouds

At the beginning of the year, immerse your students in wonderful read-alouds that are then added to the classroom library. To create an environment where students love to read and love being read to, we must make sure they regularly hear engaging fiction, nonfiction, and poetry. As we share our reading passion with our students, we will see them grow to love literature and take good care of the beautiful books in our classroom. If your school's budget is limited for classroom libraries, your school and local librarians may be excellent supports for you. Invite them to partner with you in bolstering your classroom collection by featuring library books that rotate every other week or once a month. A small sampling of some wonderful titles to start off your school year can be found in Resource 2.1 (page 113). Pam's book *What to Read When: The Books and Stories to Read With Your Child—and All the Best Times to Read Them* (Avery/Penguin, 2009) is another great read-aloud resource.

A book display sits atop clearly labeled book bins.

Leveled Books

About 20 to 30 percent of your classroom library should comprise leveled books. Leveled books have been written with the express purpose of teaching your students how to read. The print is controlled to help scaffold students' reading development. These days, there are many excellent authors writing leveled texts. While some of the stories are simple, they are building blocks to help your students learn to love to read. In the primary grades, these books have fewer words than the picture books we typically read aloud. Do not let this worry you. The books you read aloud should provide those "reach" experiences that give your children a strong sense of story and literature. The leveled books allow them to practice their reading skills. Both provide critically important foundations for your children. Keep your leveled books in clearly labeled, separate bins so your students can easily access them.

The table below lists some of the many publishing companies that sell leveled books.

Publishing Company	Web site
Abrams	www.abramslearningtrends.com
Bebop Books	www.bebopbooks.com
The Booksource	www.booksource.com
Heinemann Raintree	www.heinemannraintree.com
Mondo Publishing	www.mondopub.com
National Geographic	www.ngsp.com
Newbridge	www.newbridgeonline.com
Red Rocket Readers	www.redrocketreaders.com
Rigby	www.rigby.com
Scholastic	www.scholastic.com
Sundance	www.sundancepub.com
Wright Group	www.wrightgroup.com

Consider ordering a classroom license for the Web site *Reading A–Z.com* (www.readinga-z.com), which enables you to print out premade leveled books.

An easily accessible leveled library

Making the Most of a Small Budget

Tight school budgets are a reality most teachers face from year to year. This can make building a classroom library challenging. Here are some ways to build your library, even with a small budget.

- **Visit your local library or bookstore.**
  Local libraries have regular sales on books to make room for new books. Large bookstores have a section of picture books for a great price, and educators often get a discount on classroom purchases.

- **Scour local flea markets and garage sales.**
  People are always trying to shed books their children have outgrown. Look for flea markets and garage sales in your area.

- **Ask for donations.**
  Write a note home asking parents to donate books throughout the year to your classroom library. At the end of the year, ask your students to make donations of books they have outgrown and want to share with next year's class. A donation label (designed by you or your students) tucked inside your donated books will excite and encourage your current students to contribute.

- **Collect Scholastic points.**
  Scholastic offer great prices for teachers, and if your students buy books, you can use points to order books for your classroom.

- **Make books.**
  You and your students can make little books, based on a favorite book, poem, chant, or shared experience like a field trip.

- **Swap books.**
  Buddy up with a colleague and swap books throughout the year so you always have some new titles in your library.

- **Look for used bookstores or gently used books online**
  For a great price, you can order gently used books online through Amazon or Barnes & Noble. These books often have library bindings.

- **Be patient.**
  Allow yourself time to gather books and materials. Remember, if you make getting books a priority, your library will soon be overflowing!

Organizing Your Books

For classroom libraries to feel warm and inviting, we need to keep them organized with a system that students can understand and help to maintain. Students need easy access when choosing books, and they like to know where to return them. Students should identify the kinds of books they want to read, and know the difference between the leveled and non-leveled texts. To support our learners in knowing the difference between fiction and nonfiction, we need to teach explicitly about both kinds of books. (For more information on teaching about fiction and nonfiction, see *The Complete Year in Reading and Writing*, Grades K–2, Scholastic). We can teach our students to think about their passions and interests and support them in choosing books they want to read.

To begin, set aside some time to organize your classroom library. Leave some library space empty so the children can help you sort books and learn where things go in the library, making the space their own. Your students can be very helpful in this process at any time during the year and often have the best ideas about how to organize the library. Ask them: What would help you find books most easily? How would you categorize the books? They will invent ideas that will amaze you and make them proud!

Sorting Your Books

The first step in organizing your library is to sort your books into categories. One of the easiest ways to do this is to find a nice, large space either on the rug or floor or on a table and begin to put your books into stacks. Some common categories for books include (but are not limited to) the following: alphabet, school, holidays, specific authors, picture books, fiction, dinosaur books, fairy tales, folktales, fictional animals, land animals, space, ocean animals, food and recipes, bugs and insects, reptiles, fish, pets, famous people, family, series, magazines, books we love, favorite read-alouds, and leveled books. Be sure to ask your students for their ideas. A kindergarten class invented the "bedtime story" category. A first-grade class collected "books that surprise us." A second-grade class added the category "books about dragons!"

Materials Needed—Oh, Those Wondrous Containers!

The second step is to get plastic bins, baskets, or other containers. They can be found at a local dollar store or any of the education supplies catalogs, including, but not limited to, Lakeshore Learning, Really Good Stuff, and Classroom Direct. It is always a nice touch to have different-colored baskets or bins to add brightness to the classroom. The bins need to be large enough so the books can face forward and students can flip through them, looking at the cover and title to make a choice.

Library bins or baskets

Labeling Bins Clearly

Once we have sorted our books into categories and put them into baskets, we are ready for the next step. It is now time to label the baskets. The label should be large and easy to see and can have a picture to match, both to help students know what is in the basket and to make it aesthetically pleasing. Some teachers feel comfortable drawing the pictures themselves. However, if you are not feeling artistic, Google images offers a vast array of options, and many computer programs, such as Print Shop and Boardmaker, also include images. After you make the label, the best way to keep the label on the bin without wear and tear is to put packing tape around the label and tape it to the bin, as shown at right.

Clearly labeled bins

Labeling Books

For younger students who may have a hard time returning books to their proper place, it is helpful to have a picture or icon to guide them. One of the easiest ways to do this is to use the little reward stickers that come in all different shapes and sizes, such as smiley faces, butterflies, kites, hearts, stars, and many others. Choose a specific sticker for each book category, and put the appropriate sticker on each book as well as on the basket label (the top right corner of the front cover is best). This labeling system helps tremendously with keeping the classroom library properly organized as well as making students more independent book shoppers and returners.

Stickers on book baskets match stickers on books.

Labeling Leveled Books

The leveled books in your library also need to be clearly labeled. Two common and widely used systems are Fountas and Pinnell (levels A–Z) and DRA (levels A–60). Either of these systems works well, and we recommend them both, but choose one! For students to grow as readers, they need practice in books right at their level. The leveled texts can also have a sticker with a number or letter naming the level of the book. The bin should also be clearly labeled. Some teachers use a color system instead, to eliminate competitiveness when students are choosing from certain baskets. This is shown in the chart below. The Level A books are marked with a red 1, the Level B books are marked with a red 2, and so on.

Grade Level	Fountas/ Pinnell	DRA Level	Independent Levels	Stages
K	A	A–1	Red 1	Emergent
K–1	B	2	Red 2	Emergent
K–1	C	3, 4	Red 3	Emergent
1	D	6	Blue 1	Early
1	E	8	Blue 2	Early
1	F	10	Blue 3	Early
1	G	12	Yellow 1	Transitional
1	H	14	Yellow 2	Transitional
1	I	16	Yellow 3	Transitional
1–2	J	18	Green 1	Transitional
2	K	20	Green 2	Transitional
2–3	L	24	Green 3	Transitional
2–3	M	28	Orange 1	Extending
3	N	30, 34	Orange 2	Extending
3	O	38	Orange 3	Extending
3–4	P	38	Light Blue 1	Fluent
4	Q	40	Light Blue 2	Fluent
4	R	40	Light Blue 3	Proficient
4–5	S	40	Light Green 1	Proficient
4–5	T	44	Light Green 2	Proficient
5	U	44	Light Green 3	Proficient
5–6	V	44	Brown 1	Proficient
5–6	W	50	Brown 2	Proficient
6	X	50	Brown 3	Proficient
6	Y	50	Purple 1	Proficient
7–8	Z	60	Purple 2	Proficient

Providing for Student Independence

Now that we have created working classroom libraries with books arranged by theme, author, genre, and level, we can begin to think about how to help our students use the classroom library on their own. The more strategies we give our students to work independently, the more time we will have for small-group and individual instruction. (See Management Strategies #6 and #7 for more information on small-group and individual instruction.)

Individual Book Containers

Independent reading time is the essence of teaching students how to read. To grow as readers, students must have consistent time *every day* to read books at their level and books of interest. Each student should have a container to hold the books he or she will read during independent reading time. Here are our recommendations for book containers.

Baggies

You can use sturdy, gallon-size resealable plastic baggies for each student and organize them in table bins. This option takes up less space when you have a small classroom.

Baggies hold students' independent reading books.

Magazine Boxes

Magazine boxes are made of cardboard or plastic. Plastic magazine bins can be found at www.reallygoodstuff.com or office supply stores. If budgets are tight, students can also bring in cereal boxes, cut them to resemble magazine boxes, and cover the boxes with wrapping paper to make them festive.

Baskets or Bins

You can also use plastic baskets or bins, also found at the above sources. These are sturdy and easy for students to manage.

Once you have decided how to organize individual books, it is necessary to label them clearly with students' names. It can also be helpful to assign spots for the bags or boxes so students know exactly where to return them when they've finished using them for the day.

Number of Books

It is not necessarily the rule that the more books the better. Too many books in a container can be overwhelming for children. We recommend in kindergarten and first grade that students have up to ten books in their box. The leveled books for many students in these grades (levels A–E) are very short, so students will move through them quickly. Thus, they will need more books to increase their reading stamina (the amount of time they are able to read and the pages they can read). Included in the set of ten books may be two or three books that are also read in small-group instruction. Add these to book containers so students can continue to reread and practice the skills and strategies taught in the small group. If students in first or second grade are reading longer books, they will not need as many leveled books.

Each child should have two or three books that are interest-based and not necessarily at the student's particular reading level—they might be either challenging or easy books (above or below the child's reading level) that fit the criterion

Magazine boxes hold students' independent reading books.

Reading
Isaias

4

Student book boxes are labeled clearly with the reader's name.

of being of interest to the reader. One or two may also be comfortable favorites the student would like to reread. These books can come from anywhere in the library. For more information on helping students to make wise book choices and an extensive list of appropriate books, see the Complete Year series, Grades K–2 (Scholastic, 2008).

Create Book Swap Schedules

When choosing books, our students—especially kindergartners and first graders—need support. Students stay motivated and excited about their reading when they have a variety of books and change them once a week. Create a schedule that allows small groups of students to "book-shop" on various days. This will enable you to assist students in returning old books and in shopping for new ones. For more information on how to support your students in choosing books, see Management Strategy #5, on fostering independence.

Refreshing the Library as the Year Unfolds

As thoughtful teachers, we aim always to keep our libraries interesting and current for our students. Our libraries should directly reflect the learning in our classrooms. As a result, sections of the classroom library are often in flux, with new baskets rotating in and others rotating out. Rotate baskets of books that support seasonal and curriculum connections as well as student interests and levels. Continue throughout the year to enlist student participation in creating categories for book baskets.

Books are organized to support specific reading and writing instruction.

Gathering Books That Support Reading and Writing Instruction

As the year unfolds, the make-up of our library may change as we add baskets of books that support our specific month-by-month reading and writing instruction. If we are teaching students how to use punctuation to read fluently, we will have a basket of read-alouds that feature punctuation—books by Mo Willems, Jules Feiffer, Donald Crews, and others. If we are studying an author and the craft of his or her writing, we should have a basket of books by that author. If we are studying characters and how they affect a story, we will have a basket with strong characters, such as Tacky the Penguin books by Helen Lester or Ian Falconer's Olivia books. If we are studying narrative writing, we will have a basket of books with strong story elements, such as all the Mouse books by Kevin Henkes, or the Strega Nona series by Tomie dePaola. Students may choose these books, considered interest-based books since they are beyond what most students can read independently, for their individual containers.

Assessing the Interests and Needs of Our Students

Another way our library changes over time is based on student interest. If we know we have students who are interested in snakes, and this topic will help motivate them to read, we can create a basket of books on this topic (from our local or school library) and add it to our classroom library. We can add author bins based on student requests, and theme books for the same reason. An inexpensive way to match student interest is to exchange books with our colleagues. If you know the teacher next door has a lot of books on a topic your students love, exchange book bins, and switch back later in the year. This helps to keep our libraries interesting. The same goes for leveled books. We can switch our level A books with the teacher next door once our students have read through all of the A books in our leveled bins. This allows our students to have more choices over time, increasing stamina and interest in independent reading.

Displaying Seasonal Books

Use the library as a place to display seasonal books. Organize a special back-to-school book bin in September, or in January, a bin with books about winter. When we highlight changes to our library throughout the year, we keep our students intrigued and excited.

Adding to and Changing Books

If you have a lot of books, you may put out some of them for the first half of the year and then change them for the second half. Mid-year in first grade is a perfect time to revitalize your leveled collection by adding early chapter books and other high-interest nonfiction books. In kindergarten and second grade we also change books every other month or halfway through the year, in order to display new books and updated titles.

Classroom library with book bins clearly organized by level, topic, author, series, and genre

Make space for reference and content-area books.

The Writing Center

The writing center is an important space in the classroom that sends a strong message to our students that we value writing. The center holds the materials students use to write stories, poetry, nonfiction, song lyrics, notes, lists, and signs. Like our classroom library, our writing center should be highly accessible and clearly organized so students know where and how to get the materials they need. The center holds everything from pencils and staplers to paper and writing folders or notebooks. While it may not be the only place in your classroom where students write, it is the go-to spot for all the tools and resources they need so they can write.

Choosing Appropriate Materials

The writing center will house all the materials necessary to help our students become independent, successful writers. As we move through the grades, the materials will change to support the needs of our growing students. Below is a list of materials for your centers.

	Materials	
Kindergarten and First Grade	• one to four paper choices • blank paper for covers or drawings • writing folders organized by table • date stamps • extra erasers, pencils, markers, crayons, and colored pencils • scissors • tape • paper clips • staplers	• sticky notes • extra alphabet and blend charts • editing checklists (increasing expectations by grade) • clipboards • basket for work to be published • anchor books to show craft of writing • correction tape • laptops
Second Grade	Same as above, with the addition of the following: • three to four paper choices • writing folders or notebooks organized by groups according to where students sit • thesaurus	

These materials can be organized in small plastic baskets or bins, which are easy to find at office supply stores, dollar stores, or education supply stores.

Neatly arranged materials in a writing center

Here is the Writing Center.

Bins and trays hold materials and student folders.

Providing for Student Independence

Just as students learn to choose books independently, we want them to be able to access writing materials with ease. This allows us to spend our time conferring with students or working with small instructional writing groups. Here are ways we can help our students become independent.

Writing Folders, Notebooks, or Laptops

In kindergarten and first grade, students can use writing folders as the containers for their writing work. By second grade, students will move to writing notebooks as a place to generate ideas and write. If your school is well-equipped technologically, laptops may replace notebooks as the tool of choice. Folders and notebooks are best organized in bins, by table, as pictured below. The utility bins typically used for holding cleaning supplies are perfect for this as they have easy-to-carry handles and plenty of space to hold the folders.

The Inside and Outside of Writing Folders and Notebooks

Increase writing independence by being specific about what you help your students put on the inside and outside of writing folders. Students personalize the outside of their writing folders and notebooks with family photos, drawings, stickers, and individual words that hold special meaning for them (names of people or places). On the back of the folder it is helpful to have an alphabet chart that writers can use as a resource for conventions and writing words independently. If you are fortunate enough to have laptops, a virtual folder should contain these resources.

Inside, the folders should feature three lists: (1) word wall words, (2) topic lists, and (3) an "I am learning to" list. Individualized word walls contain the spelling words for which students are held accountable. (See Resource 2.2, My Word Wall, pages 114–116.) To this list we can add simple sight words that we are asking students to know and transfer to their writing, or individualized spelling words that come directly from their own writing.

The second is a list of topic ideas. This list can be given as homework or can be generated in school as a beginning-of-the-year writing lesson. It can be used a few times during the year to support students when thinking about ideas for their writing. (See Resource 2.3, My Writing Ideas, page 117.)

Personalized student writing folder

The last is a list of things students have been taught to do in their writing. This list grows over time as you confer with your students during independent writing time. It contains the teaching points from your conference or small instructional writing groups. It is a daily reminder of the tips and techniques, skills and strategies you've discussed with your students that they can use to make their writing stronger. (See Resource 2.4, I Am Learning to..., page 118.)

Another way to support topic generation is what we call "The Four Prompts." They are *I wonder*, *I remember*, *I observe*, and *I imagine*. With some modeling, we can easily help our children write using these prompts. They can then use them as their toolbox for generating writing ideas for years to come, selecting one or the other when they are truly "stuck." For more on teaching "The Four Prompts," see the Complete Year series (Scholastic, 2008).

For our kindergarten and first-grade students, it can also be very helpful to have red and green dot stickers, one on each side of the pocket folder. This helps students monitor front-burner work they must attend to at the moment (red) and the work that awaits them on the back burner (green). Having these resources easily accessible to students will help them with both independence and organization. For more information about writing time and student independence, see Management Strategy #5.

Refreshing the Writing Center as the Year Unfolds

Like our classroom library, the writing center should change as the year unfolds. To keep our students engaged in and enthusiastic about writing, we add fresh writing materials and other resources connected to our instruction.

Paper Choice

As we work on different aspects of our instruction, our paper choices should change. When our students are writing narratives, we might offer paper that supports the work of including characters, setting, events, and a tie-up (conclusion). When our students are writing poetry, we share paper with lines in different places on the page so students can be creative about their space. When our students are writing nonfiction, we might support their work with paper that features text boxes, spaces for headings, boxes for photos, and lines in different places on the page. For more information on genre instruction, please see the kindergarten through second-grade books in the Complete Year series.

Writing center with labeled paper choices

Editing Tools

We will also change the writing center to meet the needs of our students as they begin to get better at editing and revising their own work or at peer editing. Some of the tools to support this work include colored pencils or pens to make changes, sticky notes to make comments, and correction tape to put over words to change the spelling or the way the writing sounds. We can also make scissors and tape available to students so they can cut a picture from one page, paste it on a new piece of paper, and write new words below it. As technology becomes more of an active presence in classrooms, our students of all ages can practice revision on their laptops. These should be kept near or in the writing center as well.

Top Five Tips for Organizing Materials

1 Place stickers or photos on book baskets.

One of the ways to help our youngest learners with organization of the classroom library is to have stickers or photos on each book basket and book so they know where books can be returned. These can be small reward stickers, Boardmaker (software) pictures, pictures drawn by students, photos taken of a specific book, or even a picture from Google images that makes sense for that specific book. Here is an example of each.

- Stickers—A little butterfly can go on the basket of Nonfiction Insects, and the same reward sticker will go on each book from that basket.

- Boardmaker pictures—This software program has many different icons; for example, we can put a picture of a school on the Books About School basket and the same picture on each of the books in that basket.

- Photos—You can take a picture of a book by Mem Fox and use that photo on the Mem Fox basket, as well as on each book in the basket. For author studies, consider sticking a picture of the author on the basket and a matching one on the front cover of each book.

- Google images—We can choose an image to represent a specific category and put it on the basket, as well as on each book in that category.

2 Organize pencils by container.

Something as simple as a student needing a sharpened pencil can result in a big interruption during your small-group instruction. It is very helpful to have two coffee-can-size containers in an easily accessible place, one for sharpened pencils and one for unsharpened pencils.

Library baskets with matching stickers for basket and books

Table caddies keep supplies neat.

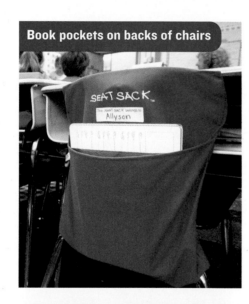
Book pockets on backs of chairs

Book box numbers correspond to numbered spots on the shelves.

3 Employ caddies for materials.

Having community supplies teaches students how to share and supports creating a working classroom community where we take care of all materials. To keep these materials organized, it works well to have a caddy at each table with materials students will need to do their daily work, including pencils, crayons, extra erasers, and scissors.

4 Hang independent book pockets on chairs.

One way to save space is to put book pockets on the backs of chairs where students can keep their independent books or other materials. These pockets are sold at school supply stores such as Lakeshore and Really Good Stuff.

5 Create numbered spots for book boxes.

One tip to help students put book boxes back in their spots is to number the book boxes and their spots on the shelves. This helps avoid disagreements that go along with putting books back in place. Everything has a place, and the place is assigned. The number on the book box matches the number on the shelf.

You Asked, We Answered

Organizing our space for learning is a key to success. Here are some common questions about staying organized.

Q My classroom is small, and I do not have room for a classroom library. What can I do?

A The classroom library is essential. Look at your space and see if there are materials and furniture that are not being used or can be moved. Put your desk against a wall to limit the amount of space it takes up in the classroom. You do not need a separate library area; the library can be portable and placed right around your meeting area. You can start small, with a few bins, and add more as needed as the year progresses, or even switch out books for new ones to update students' selections. You can also use rolling carts, as in the photo at right, that can be tucked away and then brought out during reading time.

Leveled classroom library on a rolling cart

Q I have centers around my classroom that take up a lot of space, which makes it difficult to find a place for a meeting area. What can I do?

A We recommend *moving centers*, where the material for the activity can be put away in a basket and placed at the back of the room when not in use. For example, instead of a poetry center, you can have a poetry basket that can be moved from one space to another with everything that is needed to do the activity neatly tucked inside the basket.

Movable centers in bins

Q It takes too much time to put my library together. How can I organize it quickly?

A Remember that a library can expand over time. Put your books into simple categories, as mentioned earlier in this chapter (page 28). Know that your categories don't have to be perfect right away; instead, they are a work in progress. Set monthly goals to organize one or two baskets every few weeks.

Plan for Success!

Neat and accessible classroom libraries and writing centers are essential for our students to feel comfortable engaging in the process of reading and writing. This second Great Eight strategy of organization helps us jump off into the world of learning. Our students will feel a sense of calm reassurance as we help them build skills and grow as readers and writers, knowing that everything they need is well organized for them.

Our next management strategy is all about scheduling time. Time can be our worst enemy or our best friend. Predictable calendars make a world of difference. In this next chapter, we will share with you our best tips for how to make everything work well together in a way that is not overwhelming for you or your students.

A well-organized classroom library

Scheduling Time: Daily Calendars That Work

Time flies by in the classroom. We begin our morning rituals together, and before we know it, our students are leaving for lunch. It is easy to lose track of time within the hustle and bustle of our busy classroom lives. The movie director Woody Allen once said, "Showing up is 90 percent of life." He may have been half joking, but he was on to something. Good time management is the key to effective teaching. This third Great Eight strategy will ease your mind each day. Scheduling wisely and well helps your students know what to expect, which allows them to grow toward independence.

The Flow of Our Day

Best-practice instruction typically occurs within three grouping structures: whole class, small group, and individualized. While we can all agree that these forms of instruction are essential for great teaching, it is quite another matter to fit in all the curricular content we are required to address—and to do so smoothly and successfully!

There is a continuous flow, or pattern, to the movement in our classrooms. We meet with the whole class to teach something, send students off to practice what they have learned in small groups or individually, and then reconvene the class to debrief, or wrap up, the learning experience. We call this movement "whole-small-whole" instruction, and it is an incredibly effective way to schedule each portion of your day. Whole-small-whole keeps students alert as they move through the classroom and the day. It gives them an immediate opportunity to apply what was taught or discussed during the whole-class instruction. Teachers have said to us that as they are learning to manage the flow of reading/writing instruction, they even chant "whole-small-whole" to themselves as a mantra.

This flow can be used throughout the day, not just for literacy instruction. When your kindergartners have center time, first gather them for whole-class instruction. Introduce new material, highlight student work from the previous day, or discuss what you hope to see (or not see) in a particular center. This whole-class instruction gives purpose and intention to the activities that will follow. It gives us the opportunity to demonstrate what we would like to see students try—a skill, a behavior, a tool. At the conclusion of center time, again bring your students together for wrap-up and highlight student successes. As you look at the sample schedules in this chapter, think about whole-small-whole and how it gives a predictable rhythm to the day.

Sample Schedules

Scheduling the school day is the ultimate teaching challenge. We want to fit so much in, and time is often not on our side. Here we share sample schedules and ways to fit instruction into the parameters of the school day. We realize that these schedules may not match your needs exactly; you may have more time for special area classes (e.g., music, art, library, or gym) or a longer lunch. However, the more consistent and predictable we can be with our scheduling, the more quickly students learn to transition from one activity to another, thus giving us a few precious extra minutes here and there. Use these schedules to talk with your colleagues about creating your ideal schedule. Practice creating several different options so you can get a sense of what works for you.

> ### Helpful Tip
>
> **U**sing an egg timer or digital timer during whole-group instruction, independent practice, and the wrap-up helps us all stay on schedule.

Kindergarten Sample Schedules

Some kindergarten classrooms are full day and some are half day. Here, we share with you scheduling options for both. No matter how much time you have, kindergarten is a rare and wonderful time in a child's life. The confluence of play and learning will never be stronger, and the children are in a unique and powerful moment of openness to and delight with the world, relationships, and you. Management strategies for the kindergarten classroom are vital because our children need to feel secure, comfortable, and confident navigating their new environments. They are highly eager and motivated, but the slightest sense of being off balance is going to cause behavioral issues. The more you can create warm yet highly predictable managed environments, the calmer and more joyous your experiences together will be.

Half-Day Kindergarten

8:40–9:00	Unpack and Morning Meeting Greet and discuss the day ahead, calendar activities, read-aloud
9:00–9:20	Word Work or Shared Reading (alternate days)
9:20–9:50	Reading Time or Writing Time (every other day or alternate weeks) Whole-class lesson, small-group and independent practice, whole-class wrap-up
9:50–10:20	Math
10:20–10:30	Break/Snack
10:30–11:15	Special Class (Music, Art, Gym, Library)
11:15–11:35	Center Time (also known as purposeful play)
11:35–11:45	Read-Aloud Dismissal

Full-Day Kindergarten

8:40–9:00	Unpack and Morning Meeting Greet and discuss the day ahead, calendar activities, read-aloud
9:00–9:20	Word Work Whole-class lesson, small-group center activities, whole-class wrap-up
9:20–9:35	Shared Reading Using a big book or poem to teach students reading skills and strategies
9:35–9:45	Read-Aloud, Singing, or Story-Telling
9:45–10:25	Writing Whole-class lesson, small-group and independent practice, whole-class wrap-up
10:25–10:40	Break/Snack
10:40–11:20	Reading Whole-class lesson, small-group and independent practice, whole-class wrap-up
11:20–12:00	Special Class (Music, Art, Gym, Library)
12:00–1:00	Lunch and Recess
1:00–1:30	Math Whole-class lesson, small-group and independent practice, whole-class wrap-up
1:30–2:00	Center Time (also known as purposeful play)
2:00–2:30	Science or Social Studies (alternate days)
2:30–2:40	End-of-the-Day Meeting Discussion, singing, and/or read-aloud
2:40–2:45	Pack Up and Dismissal

Kindergartners at work in writing spots

First-Grade Sample Schedule

First graders are ready for more independence. But they are still so young. The Great Eight can help them stay on course while giving them opportunities to explore their own learning worlds. First graders are losing teeth, having baby siblings, tying shoes, putting on their backpacks, reading books of their choice. They are feeling a lot like big kids, but they also have an urge to put their thumbs in their mouths when they get tired. Scheduling is critical to helping them build pathways to independence that feel joyous and secure.

First-Grade Sample Schedule

8:40–9:00	Unpack and Morning Meeting Greet and discuss the day ahead, calendar activities, read-aloud
9:00–9:15	Read-Aloud
9:15–9:30	Partner Reading Students meet with a partner to look at one book together, sharing the book and talking about it.
9:30–9:45	Shared Reading
9:45–10:30	Reading Time Whole-class instruction, small-group and independent practice, whole-class wrap-up
10:30–10:45	Word Work
10:45–11:00	Break/Snack
11:00–11:45	Special Class (Music, Art, Gym, Library)
11:45–12:30	Writing Time Whole-class instruction, small-group and independent practice, whole-class wrap-up
12:30–1:30	Lunch and Recess
1:30–2:15	Math Whole-class instruction, small-group and independent practice, whole-class wrap-up
2:15–2:45	Social Studies/Science/Center Time (alternate)
2:45–2:55	Pack Up and Goodbye Meeting
2:55–3:00	Dismissal

Second-Grade Sample Schedule

Your second graders are well on their way to building independence in their learning lives, but they are not there yet. Packing up at the end of the day can still be overwhelming, and sometimes we overload them with many directions at once, thinking they are older than they are. Take careful steps with your students, using your schedule as a way to model for them that you value routines. If we are explicit, they will pay close attention to routines in class, and mirror that predictability at home. A great schedule is the key to establishing the foundations for good work habits that will last them their whole lives.

8:40–9:00	Unpack and Morning Meeting Greet and discuss the day ahead, calendar activities, read-aloud
9:00–9:15	Read-Aloud
9:15–9:30	Partner Reading/Book Clubs Students meet with a partner to share and discuss books or participate in mini book clubs where they are all reading and discussing the same book.
9:30–9:45	Shared Reading Two to three times a week; on alternate days, schedule longer partner time.
9:45–10:30	Reading Time Whole-class instruction, small-group and independent practice, whole-class wrap-up
10:30–10:45	Word Work
10:45–11:30	Writing Time Whole-class instruction, small-group and independent practice, whole-class wrap-up
11:30–12:15	Special Class (Music, Art, Gym, Library)
12:15–1:15	Lunch and Recess
1:15–2:00	Writing Time Whole-class instruction, small-group and independent practice, whole-class wrap-up
2:00–2:45	Social Studies/Science
2:45–2:55	Pack Up and Goodbye Meeting
2:55–3:00	Dismissal

Top Five Tips for Scheduling Time

It's one thing to create a daily schedule for your class and another to actually stick to it! Here are five tips to help you use your time efficiently.

1 Stick to the time you have for each activity.

We all feel the pressure of time. Also, when something is going well we often want to extend it. Try to keep the schedule consistent as much as possible. If you have 40 minutes for reading, stick to 40 minutes. If you have ten minutes of independent writing time, stay within the limit. Our more challenged students may feel cheated when you say: "You did so well, so let's go longer!" For them, getting to the end of those minutes successfully was a big achievement. They hit the goal you established for them; now you need to hold up your end of the bargain and keep your promise to move on to the next learning experience.

2 Tighten up transitions.

The more quickly and effectively we can move our students from one activity to another, the less time we will lose during transitions. Teach students how to transition from one activity to another in the same way you teach other important skills. For more on transitions and routines, see Management Strategy #4.

3 Post the daily schedule.

Post your schedule in a visible place in the classroom. Include the times for each activity to help you stay on schedule.

4 Review the schedule each morning.

Read the schedule with your students each morning so they will know what to expect for the day. This will help them transition quickly from one activity to the next.

5 Plan with intention.

Creating schedules, planning instruction, and gathering appropriate materials ahead of time will ensure time is spent well. If you move efficiently from one part of the day to the next, your students will as well.

Well-managed time and well-organized space are essential ingredients in the recipe for success.

You Asked, We Answered

Q How do I fit everything into a half-day kindergarten schedule?

A One option is to do three days of reading instruction and two days of writing, or vice versa. Another is to combine your reading and writing instruction into one block of time. An example of this would be students learning to read labels in books, while also writing their own label books. For more reading/writing teaching examples, check out *The Complete Year in Reading and Writing, K,* by Karen McNally and Pam Allyn.

Q How many times a week do I need to teach reading and writing?

A To get better at anything, we need to practice. The more often we give our children opportunities to read and write, the stronger our students will become as readers and writers.

A teacher confers with writers, providing individual support.

Time Is of the Essence

Time and our own unique tastes create the "just-right blend" that makes our classrooms special places to be. This third Great Eight strategy, scheduling, sets us up for the fourth—the establishment of routines that will make transitions throughout the day easier for you. The blending of a strong schedule and predictable routines is a winner in any classroom.

Establishing Routines: Rituals and Transitions

We can lean on our routines; they create a known and predictable path through the day. Our students will appreciate the routines we set up for them as well. They will appreciate knowing what comes next and what is expected of them. Once routines are in place, you can take a step back from managing students and focus on teaching. Children thrive on predictability that is matched with a vibrant curriculum and the impact of your own inspirations. Just as they love bedtime stories and the familiar sound of beloved voices, so, too, in school the routines they come to expect every day make it easier for you and them to savor time.

Daily Routines

Our students do their best work when they know what to expect. The more consistent we are, the more our students will succeed. The way our day looks in the classroom can be predictable without being at all dull. We can create a flow to the day that allows our students to feel prepared, but also allows us to make each day special and unique.

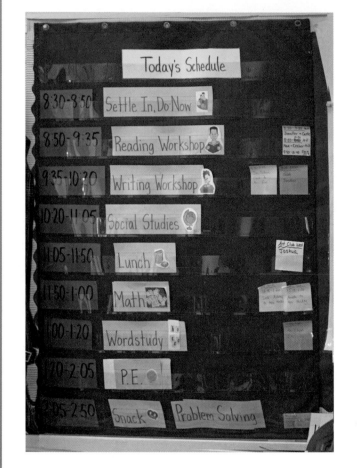

Consistent Schedules

When our youngest students come into the room, the first thing they notice is the daily schedule (see sample at left). They are quick to run to the spot where we keep this information and talk about the day's events. If there is a change in the daily routine, they are the first to notice. You may hear "Where is partner reading today?" or "Why is writing workshop after lunch?" Our students are flexible, but they also thrive on consistency. When students know what is coming next, it reduces their transition time to a new activity.

Unpacking and Packing Up

Here are some helpful tips for making your day run smoothly.

Use a timer.

Just as we use a timer for teaching and independent practice, we also use one for unpacking at the start of the school day and packing up when it's time to go home. Challenge your students: Give them more time at the beginning of the year, and, as the year continues, snip back the allotted time.

Give awards.

We give awards for our reading, writing, and partner time, and similarly we can also give awards for unpacking and packing up to help motivate our students to move a little more quickly. (See Resource 4.1, Unpacking and Packing Up awards, page 119.) To be equitable, keep track of who has already received an award.

Provide baskets for finished work and notes from home.

Have two baskets, one for notes from home, and one for finished work, where students can put their homework. Then, when you have some time during the day, you know where to go to check these notes and homework.

Be very explicit.

Do not take it for granted that your students know how to unpack and pack up. Demonstrate unpacking and packing up yourself—model every action. Show students how to get their folders and put their mail away, how to get their bags and put the folders inside. Be clear about where everything goes. As a resource, display an anchor chart with routines.

Finished work and note baskets

Our Unpacking Routine

- Bring your backpacks to your seat.
- Pull out your take-home folder.
- Put your notes from home in the note basket and your homework in the homework basket.
- Put your folder in your cubby.
- Unpack your books.
- Put your books back in the correct library basket or your book box.
- Take out your snack and put it in your cubby.
- Hang your book bag and coat on your hook.

Whole-group instruction

Whole-Group Instruction

Whole-group instruction is also predictable. When you gather together, students know that it is their turn to listen and your turn to teach. Give your students specific spots on the rug. This helps eliminate the minor distraction of deciding where to sit (and next to whom). Decide on your routine for whole-class instruction and follow it each time students are gathered together.

The purpose of whole-group literacy instruction is to demonstrate some aspect of being a reader or writer. For whole-group reading and writing time, we recommend 5 to 15 minutes of direct, explicit instruction. After 15 minutes, students will have a hard time staying engaged in your instruction. Movement among the three grouping structures (whole-small-whole) will help you keep your students highly engaged and focused, allowing them to internalize your whole-class instruction more effectively.

Engagement Strategies

Here are some strategies to keep your students actively engaged during whole-group instruction.

Use key phrases or questions.

Use key phrases such as "Yesterday we learned..., and today I am going to teach you..." as soon as you begin the lesson to clarify the instruction and alert students to your intentions up front. Before sending students off to independent practice, we say, "Your job for today is..." or "Your reading/writing work for today is..." By ending this way, we are clarifying our instruction before we send students to independent practice.

Create sky or rug writers.

Invite one child at a time to write in front of the class on chart paper or another writing surface visible to the class. To involve all students in a shared writing activity, we create "sky writers" or "rug writers." Following their classmates's lead, children use their index fingers to write in the sky or on the rug.

Use dry-erase boards.

This concept is similar to the sky/rug writers. While one student may be writing in front of the class on chart paper or on a interactive whiteboard, we ask all students to write the designated word or words on a dry-erase board.

Establish "turn and talk" partners.

Rather than asking a question and inviting *one* student to answer, pose a question and ask *all* students to think about the answer. Then, have students turn and talk to a previously designated partner. This keeps all students actively engaged, involved, and accountable in the instruction. For example, we may teach students that one way to find writing ideas is to use the prompt "I remember. . . ." We model using this prompt to think of writing topics, then say to our students, "Now I want you to practice using this prompt to find writing ideas. Say, "I remember. . ." to yourself and allow memories of people or events or places to come to you. [*Give students thinking time before continuing.*] Now turn and talk to your partner about your writing ideas." When we ask students to turn and talk, they are able to practice a skill, strategy, or behavior with your assistance while giving you the opportunity to assess student understanding. Give students only a couple of minutes to talk with a partner. It is a quick chance to try out this new learning.

Students working with dry-erase boards

Turn-and-talk partners

Lead a variety of choral readings.

When doing shared reading with students, use some of the following ways to choral-read:

- read in a whisper voice
- read in a giant voice
- have girls read; have boys read
- sing the words

The variety of readings entertains the students and keeps them alert as they listen to the changing directions.

Classroom Rituals

A ritual is defined as a practice or pattern of behavior regularly performed in a set manner. We all have rituals in our own lives, and there are some wonderful rituals that set a positive classroom tone.

Bells

Collect different bells—small bells and larger bells—and use them for different purposes. A small, cheery bell sound indicates that the group is gathering. A deeper, richer sound indicates that it is time for lunch. Souvenir shops often sell bells cheaply, and it is fun to have the children decide which bell will represent which transition.

Morning Song

Children never tire of predictable songs. One of our favorites is the "good morning song" sung to the tune of "Goodnight, Ladies." It is simple: "Good morning, ____; Good morning, ____; Good morning, ____, we're glad you came." The children sing it in a circle so you can fill in each of their names as you sing.

Goodbye Song

You can use any number of tunes as your goodbye song. A beautiful one we know is "Goodbye, so long, farewell, my friends, goodbye, so long, farewell. We'll see you soon again, my friends, so goodbye, so long, farewell." But really, any lovely little song is enough, even the "ABC song." Your children will leave the room humming and happy.

Line-Up Song

When we ask students to line up, we can sing, "Are we ready, is everybody ready, is everybody ready to go to lunch? [*or substitute wherever you are going*] Jenny is ready and so is Max, and so is Shontay and so is Michael." This encourages students to get in line quietly and show you they are ready to leave the classroom. Or we can sing, "Line up, line up, everybody line up, line up, line up, right now, please."

Transitions

Our classroom transition times are some of the most important routines of our day. The longer our transitions, the more instruction time we lose. Our days are full, our curriculum is rich, and we have so much to do together! The tighter our transitions, the more time we will have for instruction. Here are some ways to tighten up your time so you can create a complete day.

Create Specific Spaces for Materials

"A place for everything and everything in its place." This phrase, first cited in print in 1827, and attributed to the Reverend C. A. Goodrich, certainly applies to the classroom. Giving thoughtful consideration to where everything is in the room will help you minimize your transition time. When we set up places for writing folders, book boxes, or baggies, and even our students' "sitting spots," we move more quickly through transition time and into our instruction and independent practice. Give students spots where they sit on the rug during instruction. Give students space for their book boxes or baggies by numbering the spot on the shelf with a matching number on their book box. Organize writing folders for each table by placing them in bins, so that each student has a place to put writing. The goal is that students are able to find what they need and know where to put it back quickly and efficiently, allowing more time for instruction and independent practice.

Writing folders organized in table caddies

Book baggies organized by table

Prepare Student Book Baggies or Boxes

Before students come to the class meeting area for a whole-class lesson, they take their individual book baggies or boxes and place them where they will be doing their independent reading following the group instruction.

Assign Turn-and-Talk Partners

During whole-class instruction, we ask students to practice or process with a partner what we have just taught. When we assign turn-and-talk partners ahead of time, students do not have to worry about who will be their partner for this activity. Turn-and-talk partners change every two to six weeks.

Use an Elapsed Timer

Elapsed timers allow students to see how much time remains for a particular activity. A red indicator moves as time passes, giving students a great visual understanding of time and when an activity will be ending.

Go Directly to the Rug for Wrap-Up

After independent practice, as we transition from small to whole again, do not have students clean up their independent reading or writing right away. Have students come right to the rug for the lesson sum-up and end-of-day wrap-up, and then go back to clean up their spots. This will ensure that all students are on the rug for this important sum-up of the day's work and not lingering to clean up their reading and writing work, thus missing the important lesson conclusion and reflection.

Top Five Tips for Setting Up Routines and Managing Transitions

1 **Keep your schedule as consistent as possible.**

Start your day the same way, followed by the same activity. For example, start with the morning meeting, followed by a read-aloud, partner reading, shared reading, and so on.

2 **Sing as a way to signal a transition.**

Singing is an effective and joyful way to transition your students from one activity to another. One song you'll all enjoy: "The more we get together, together, together, the more we get together, the happier we'll be."

3 **Turn a rain stick to signal a transition.**

The gentle, musical sound of a rain stick is so soothing. We have found it to be a calming and effective way to signal to students that a transition will be taking place.

4 **Play music.**

Turn on some soothing or peppy music, depending on the need. In one of our favorite first-grade classrooms, songs such as "Here Comes the Sun," by the Beatles, played at the end of every writing period, serve as closure and indicate what we want students to do next. The children hear the song and instantly know it is time to start cleaning up, lining up, or going to their spot. We don't have to say a word about transitions by mid-October, because the students know the songs signal transition.

5 **Read aloud.**

Signal transition time by reading a short poem or a familiar picture book as students move from one place to another. Reading will keep students engaged and peaceful as they line up or move from the rug to their seats.

You Asked, We Answered

Q I like the idea of "turn-and-talk" partners, but I'm not sure my students could handle that routine. How can I ensure that they will understand how to do it?

A Bring in a colleague to help model this practice. Show your students exactly how to turn to one another, knee-to-knee, eye-to-eye. For the first several days of school, practice the motions of the turn-and-talk routine even more than the talk itself. Let the talk part last just a few seconds while you linger over the turning and the arranging of students' positions so that the turning part becomes so smooth they do it right away.

List of partners, with magnetic tape for easy movability

Q What if my students don't concentrate well in their independent reading and writing spots?

A You may have to experiment a bit with where your students feel most comfortable and are most productive as readers and writers. You may want to say that you are going to practice with writing spots for two days. Have students pick spots; then you will visit those spots and observe how comfortable and productive your students are in them. At the end of the two days, you could have students switch spots, watch them carefully, and then after four days go by, make your determination as to where they will be for the next six weeks. If you take these small choices seriously, your children will, too.

A Thriving Community Supports Independence

This fourth Great Eight strategy, the focus on routines, brings your teaching into sharp and clear focus. Rather than focus on the distractions of children not knowing where to go, when to go, or what to do, the primary focus becomes the teaching points. All those many distractions will fall away as your rituals all angle toward one thing: creating a happy, healthy learning community.

Let us now take a close look at the Great Eight strategy #5: Fostering Independence. We've done a lot of work on creating the whole-class environment that will help your students flourish. Now it is time to look at our individual students and nurture their potential for success.

Fostering Independence: Students Who Can Work on Their Own

Just as a parent celebrates every small step—the tying of a shoe, the first day of school—each day as teachers we celebrate those special moments when our students demonstrate they can do more on their own.

Our students need the time to take their own small steps toward independence. We can prepare them for this independent time by demonstrating and practicing the different activities that we would like them to do when they are working on their own. By helping our

A small group of students working with a teacher

students learn to work independently, we are scaffolding their experience and allowing them the necessary practice as readers and writers. While they are working independently, we can now work with small instructional groups or confer with students to teach reading and writing skills and strategies one-on-one.

Creating a Working Noise Level

Our primary students are social creatures. It's not surprising that the noise level in a classroom can escalate quickly. We must teach students the importance of creating a classroom with a "learning hum" (versus a "learning roar")—a classroom where transitions move smoothly, when students are working productively, immersed in an energizing working buzz. We achieve this through positive reinforcement and the creation of workspaces that enable our students to be successful. Here are some specific ways to help students understand and create a successful classroom with a working noise level.

Working in a Quiet Bubble

The language "working in a quiet bubble with a one-inch voice'" is useful to describe what the classroom sounds like during independent reading and writing time. Students will not naturally know what this means, but we can teach them how to do this.

Here is a sample lesson using the "quiet bubble":

"Every person in this classroom is a reader . . . that is so very exciting! As readers, we must read books every day so our reading muscles can get stronger and stronger. Let's think about some of the places you may see people reading. One of those places may be the library—the public library or the school library. At the library there is a rule that readers need to be very, very quiet so that people in the library can concentrate and relax and read. It is also really important to read quietly in our classroom so that others can concentrate and the teacher can work with kids in the room. I am going to teach you a way that can help you remember how to read quietly so that your friends can concentrate and so I can work with each of you every day as readers and writers.

"Does anyone know what this is?" (Show a picture of a bubble from a book or one you have drawn). "This is a bubble. Think about what it would be like to be inside this bubble; do you think it is really noisy or really quiet? If it was noisy inside I bet the bubble would pop! When you are reading today, I want you to pretend you are inside a bubble, a quiet bubble. You don't want the bubble to pop, so make sure you are extra quiet so the children around you can't hear you and you can focus on your book from inside your quiet bubble. The goal is to use a one-inch voice inside your quiet bubble, a tiny voice.

"Everyone put your arms up very slowly and pretend you are in your quiet bubble. Watch me try it. Now, you try it.

Quiet bubble whole-group lesson

"Remember, your reading work today is to read inside your quiet bubble using a one-inch voice. The children who read quietly in their quiet bubble will get a quiet bubble reading award! The best way to become a strong reader is to concentrate and read inside your bubble!" (See Resource 5.1, Quiet Bubble Award, page 120.)

With our second graders, we expect the practice of working quietly in kindergarten and first grade to transfer quickly after a few refresher lessons. As students become stronger, more fluent readers and writers, it is natural that they begin to read silently and write quietly. You may want to videotape your class so they can watch themselves and determine how well the quiet bubble is working. You can visit other classrooms to observe the noise levels and discuss with your students how you want your own classroom to sound. *Ruby Sings the Blues* by Niki Daly is a picture book that can be used to facilitate a discussion on noise levels in the classroom. Ruby, the main character, has a naturally loud voice, and throughout the course of the book she learns when it is okay to use a loud voice and when she must "turn it down."

We can't expect young children to be completely silent as they read and write. However, we can work together to create a working buzz or productive hum that feels comfortable for everyone—one that allows students to focus on their reading and writing work. The term "one-inch voice" is also extremely helpful. Our students understand the visual of one inch and they can show you with their finger and thumb precisely how big that is. It helps them to have a visual because when adults say "Be quiet!" they often think they ARE being quiet! The reminder of the one-inch voice helps them to visualize just what you mean by *quiet.*

Using Time Wisely

We have already mentioned that a helpful tool to promote increased reading and writing stamina is a timer. We set a timer for our students so they know how much time they have for independent reading and writing. It is absolutely essential that our students are reading and writing independently every day. The more students know about what they are expected to do, and for how long, the more successful they are. They are reassured by knowing there is a beginning and a predictable ending to their independent work time. This routine supports all learners. For our vulnerable learners, this concreteness helps them know how much time they have left so that they can understand and work toward predictable outcomes. For some students, if they are not sure when an activity is going to end, they become anxious and may engage in behavior that's distracting to others. If we are respectful of our students' need to know what is happening next and for how long, they are more respectful of the classroom expectations. The key here is to add minutes to independent reading and writing as the year goes on.

Each day and each month, we can add more minutes as our children become more confident and capable, while keeping in mind what is age-appropriate for each grade. The chart below shows the reading and writing expectations for each grade level by the end of the school year.

Grade Level	Student Reading Time	Student Writing Time
Kindergarten	10–15 minutes	10–20 minutes (writing/drawing)
First Grade	10–20	10–20
Second Grade	20–30	20–25

Students also learn to keep on reading or writing until time is up; they are not finished until the timer rings. Give students many options for how to do this, because when they get stuck, they are usually genuinely stuck. For example, some students believe that what you mean is that they must continue on the same writing topic, even if they are finished and the timer has not rung. In fact, you can encourage them to start a new piece if they finish their first one ahead of schedule. The same goes for reading. They don't have to stick with one book for the entire time! They should have enough books in their book boxes so that in one reading period they can make changes and explore different options as needed.

Designating Work Spaces

We can help our students be successful throughout our reading and writing time by supporting them in making wise decisions about where they will work—places where they can concentrate and focus on the task at hand. Even in the smallest of classrooms, we can find places for our students to work without too many distractions.

Reading Spots

When we assign reading and writing spots to our kindergarten and first-grade children, we are able to decrease distractions by strategically placing students in specific places. Because we take full advantage of the entire room, students have more space physically and therefore are less likely to be distracted by other readers—allowing them to increase their stamina and independence. Over time we hope to teach children to become more independent and to allow them to choose their own spots, with the expectation that they will find places where they can do their best work.

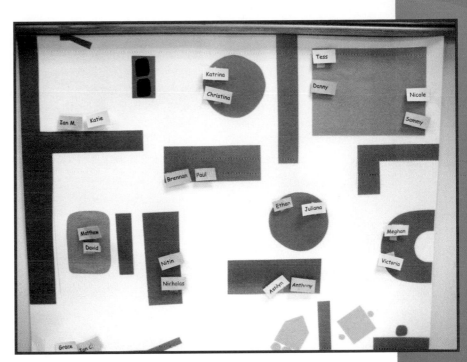

Classroom reading spots map

First graders who have learned to be reflective about their work and their habits are able to say they would rather work at a table than on the rug. Children who are given the opportunity to reflect on the importance of space come to know it is hard to work near other students when working independently and will adjust. By second grade, allow your students to choose their own reading spots. If they have been practicing independence since kindergarten, they will be able to make wise decisions about what works best for them. The important thing is that you are working on this, making decisions you think are best, and including your students as "researchers" in this process. It may seem incidental in comparison to the enormous work you will do with your students in comprehension and phonics, but, in truth, fostering student independence is just as essential.

Writing Spots

It is most common during writing time for students to work at their tables, but there are some children who may be more successful working in quiet places around the room. Provide children with clipboards (or laptops, where possible) so they can work on their writing independently in different parts of the room. It is natural that some students work best when they do not have too many distractions. The clipboards give us the opportunity to help them move to spots that will be most comfortable for them as they build independence.

How to Manage the Books

There are a few ways to manage books in the boxes and baggies. One option is to have one book-shopping day for the whole class. The children can come in groups to the library and switch their books with your support, especially in kindergarten and first grade. The second option is for groups of students in your class to each have a book-swap day. With this schedule, one group of students goes to the library each day of the week to exchange books. For example:

Monday	Tuesday	Wednesday	Thursday	Friday
James	Eric	Kevin	Jose	Bob
Lisa	Samuel	Leo	Kyle	Max
Rachel	Jeri	Alyssa	Danielle	Mary
Jenny	Greg	Omar	Alexa	Katie
Melissa	Pam	Peter	Devon	Ryan

On the specific day of the week, the students listed swap their books with teacher guidance. This can be done during a transition time, first thing in the morning, as a center during center time, or at another time during the day. It is important that the time to swap does not take place when you are leading small-group instruction, as this will take away from your time reading with your students.

The third way to manage book swapping is to teach your students to do this independently, especially in first and second grade. In order to do this successfully we need to actively teach our children:

- why choosing new books is important
- how to choose books that are at their level
- when to choose books
- how to stay with a book for a period of time

Students reading from independent book boxes

One way to support students in learning how to choose their own books is to give them what we call a *book card*. This index card, which slips into students' book boxes or baggies, lists their name and their current book level. If you use stickers on these book cards to indicate readers' current level, they peel off easily and can be replaced as students move to the next level.

Student Materials That Inspire Independence

Make sure your students are truly accountable for their work. Ask your students to keep records of their reading and writing work each day. Younger students can use simple forms to record the numbers of books they have read and to reflect on how they worked as partners through the use of emoticons such as smiley faces. Older students can keep a reading plan, keeping track of the titles read or of pages read in a chapter book. The materials we share with our students will help them build independence as well. Here are some useful examples.

Reading Records

During reading time, ask your students to keep a record of the reading work they are doing. In kindergarten, reading plans can demonstrate early reading stamina. Students reflect on how long they can read and what to do when they think they are finished, even when reading time is not yet over. You can also ask students in kindergarten to record how many books they have read and use a simple checklist to assess their use of reading workshop time. (See Resource 5.2, My Reading Checklist, page 120.)

Student filling out a reading record

In first grade we begin to ask our students to keep track of their reading work on a reading record—listing the titles of the books they read. If there are children who struggle with motor skills, have them just write the first letter of the title of each book. The purpose of this plan is to help children become aware of how they are using their reading time, to be accountable for their work, and to give you a way to monitor their reading work. The children will find a reflection system at the bottom of the reading record that asks them if they have used their reading time well and used a one-inch voice. Reading records help with management and student focus during independent work time. Provide each student with a fresh Reading Workshop Record (Resource 5.3, page 121) each day and have them circle the day of the week, to support them as they learn to read and spell the days of the week.

Second graders are learning to be independent readers. The kinds of records we want them to keep may be more about number of pages read in a book, the genre, and/or the comfort level of a book (downhill, level, or uphill). Use these records to help students reflect on themselves as readers and to set goals that will make them stronger. (See Resource 5.4, My Reading Record, page 122.)

Writing Checklists

As young writers work during writing time, we can inspire independence by having paper choices ready for them. Writing checklists remind students of their job during writing time and what to do when they finish one piece. A writing checklist can include the following.

Writing Checklist

Check off what you did below:

☐ I wrote my name.

☐ I wrote the date.

☐ I added more to my pictures or words.

☐ I reread my writing to make sure it makes sense.

Partner reading behavior chart

Partner Rubrics

One of the best ways to help our children become active readers who are thinking and talking about books is to have them work in partnerships. In partnerships, students can talk about their reading and share reading time with one another. Step one in partnership instruction is teaching what it looks like and sounds like: where to sit with a partner, how to sit, and how to treat partners kindly and fairly. Step two is instructing partners on how to talk about books. This instruction happens in all three grade levels, but can begin in kindergarten by showing a favorite part of the book and talking about why it is a favorite. We can help our students become more independent during this time by giving them partner plans to use while working with their classmates.

The first rubric (see Resource 5.5, Partner Reading, page 123) will help students to think about what partnerships look like and sound like. The instructional language to support this first rubric may be about sitting knee to knee and shoulder to shoulder, taking turns, using a one-inch voice, looking at one book together, talking about the book, and sitting in a quiet bubble. In kindergarten we can use pictures on a bookmark to represent each idea, in first grade we can add the words to the pictures, and in second grade we can change the focus to what to talk about instead of how to work together (see Resource 5.6, Partner Talk, page 124). Students are asked to reflect on their partner work each day.

Teacher Materials That Inspire Independence

Another way to support our students in becoming independent learners is to offer incentives. Young students love to please and are eager to do well in school. The more we reinforce positive behaviors, the more we can expect our students to work well during reading and writing time.

Awards

We offer awards to our students for the behaviors we are expecting during independent time. These include rewards for being strong partners, for reading stamina, for being reading- and writing-workshop stars, and even awards for working in a quiet bubble. These small paper awards mean so much to children. It is best to give them at the end of partner reading, independent reading, and independent writing. It is also helpful to keep track of which students are getting awards so that we can make sure that all of the students in the class get an award at one time or another. (See Resource 5.7, Partner Award, page 125; Resource 5.8, Strong Reader Award, page 125; Resource 5.9, Reading Workshop Award, page 126; Resource 5.10, Writing Workshop Award, page 126.)

Bookmarks

Teacher-made bookmarks can help our students become more independent. These bookmarks, differentiated for kindergarten and first grade, remind students what they can do to increase stamina during independent reading time. They have icons to support the steps children use when they are reading, such as making sure to read until time is up, rereading, looking closely at pictures, and using other strategies to increase stamina and independence. (See Resources 5.11 and 5.12, Reading Long and Strong Bookmarks, page 127.)

Visual Reminders of Reading and Writing Work

Pictures and charts are very effective in reminding students of their roles and responsibilities during independent time. These charts (see above) are visual reminders of what was taught in previous lessons and what you are expecting students to practice on their own. When students are confused or unaware of their responsibilities, they can reference the charts. In kindergarten, the chart is mostly visual, a photo of what we are asking students to do. In first and second grade, we can make a chart using words with some picture support. At the end of a writing conference, we can also place sticky notes in writing folders to remind students what we have asked of them.

Book Hospital

When our students find books that are ripped or broken, they are always eager to let you know right away. Often, we are in the middle of small-group instruction, and students have found a book in their book box that needs some taping, stapling, or gluing. A quick way to alleviate the interruptions is to create a book hospital—a basket or box in your classroom where students know they can put the books that may need a little mending and TLC.

Bin for Lost Books

We know how hard you have worked with your students to create a beautiful, organized classroom library. We also know that young students are always in a rush to put things away and move on to the next activity. As a result, books often end up in the wrong place in the classroom library (you might find a nonfiction dinosaur book in the "Books About School" bin). To support our students who are not sure where books go back, we suggest creating a "Help, I'm Lost" book basket or bin. This way, when students are returning books to the classroom library, if they are not sure where to return it, they slip it into the "Help, I'm Lost" bin. Then either you or your students can be in charge each day of making sure these books go back to the correct spots.

Sample Lessons to Inspire Independence

If we want our students to be independent, we need to teach them how to be independent. We cannot forget how young they are, nor how much they need our explicit guidance every step of the way. Model the behaviors and attitudes you want to see reflected in your students, and encourage the small and positive behaviors we often take for granted. Show your students what to do when there is a broken pencil and how to find a new one. Teach them what to do when they are finished reading the books in their book box or baggie but the timer is still going. Demonstrate how to read for a longer period of time, how to work in partnerships, and what to do when they are finished during writing time. We cannot take anything for granted. It is critical that we think through every challenge that might arise, model acceptable solutions, and support our students in all ways so they can eventually become independent problem solvers.

Below are some sample lessons to inspire independence. These lessons are taught to the whole group, and then students practice in reading or writing partnerships, depending on the lesson.

Sample Lesson: Working With Our Reading Partners

We are all readers in this classroom. One thing that readers do is read with a friend so they can think and talk about books. Today we are going to learn how to share our quiet bubble with a friend.

Now, instead of being in a bubble by yourself, you are going to be in a bubble with your partner. You and your partner are going to read together, look at one book together, sit knee-to-knee and shoulder-to-shoulder, sit in your quiet bubble, and use a one-inch voice. Watch me as I sit with _____, and see how we are sitting as partners. We are sitting knee-to-knee and shoulder-to-shoulder, and we have one book that we are looking at together.

Have two students model this work as well.

Your reading work today is to practice reading in your quiet bubble with your reading partner. Remember, you are going to sit knee-to-knee and shoulder-to-shoulder, look at one book together, and spend some time with a book. It is fun to be able to share a book with a friend and notice things in the book together! I will be looking for the children who are reading well together for a partner award.

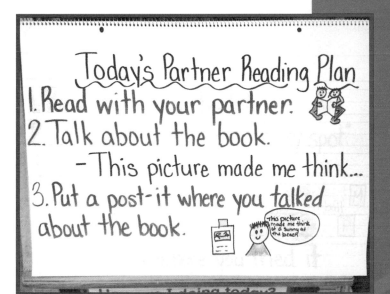

Today's Partner Reading Plan
1. Read with your partner.
2. Talk about the book.
   - This picture made me think...
3. Put a post-it where you talked about the book.

Sample Lesson: Reading Stamina

Yesterday we read for four whole minutes in our quiet bubbles, and you did an amazing job! Today we are going to learn something that readers do to make them even stronger. We are going to look at the pictures first, because that is something that strong readers do.

One thing that really helps us as readers is to look at the pictures in a book, or take a picture walk. When we look at the pictures first and say what we see, it helps us with the words when we go back to read the book. It makes us stronger as readers. Let's look at this Big Book together and see what we notice in the pictures first; then we can go back and read when we finish with the pictures.

Model using a new Big Book; tell what is happening in the pictures first. Have students try this with you, helping you tell what you see in the pictures in the book.

Now that we have looked at the pictures first and shared what we saw, we can read the words in the book, using what we remember from the pictures to help us.

Your reading work today is to read from your book baggies, but before you read the actual words, you can take a picture walk like we just did together. This helps you to become a stronger reader. Today we will set the timer again, but for five whole minutes!

In a lesson such as the one above, the goal is to continue this work so that our students' stamina increases over time. Each day we can add more minutes to the timer so that students can begin to read and write for longer periods of time during independent practice.

Sample Lesson: How to Get Writing Ideas

We are learning how writers are very thoughtful about choosing topic ideas. Today we are going to look at a poet that I love and think about how she may have discovered her ideas.

In this poetry book, Under the Sunday Tree, *Eloise Greenfield wrote poems about lots of different things. Let's look at some of the things she wrote about.*

Read a few of the poems and model thinking about the title of the poems and her choices as a writer.

Talk with your partner about Eloise and what you know about her as a writer.

Pause for a few minutes so students can talk with their partners.

Eloise Greenfield found her ideas by thinking about things that were important to her, and by using her own life experiences. That is what authors do. In my writing folder, I have a story about _____. It is a place I go that is very important to me, so it is easy for me to write about.

Take a minute to close your eyes and think about something that is important to you. Turn to the person next to you, describe it, and talk about it. This is something that you can write about.

Your writing work today is to think of some things that are important to you, that have happened to you in your life. Those are things writers write about, so think of those things and write them down in a list. Remember, all you have to do is think of things that are important to you or some experiences you have had. That will give you great writing ideas!

Sample Lesson: What to Do When You Are Finished Writing—Adding More to Your Words or Pictures

You are all writers in this class, and you've been writing stories. Today we are going to learn about what writers do when they are finished.

Sometimes when we are writing we feel that we are finished with our writing work. Today I am going to teach you some things you can do when you think you are done. Writers are never finished with their writing work. One thing that writers do is reread their writing to see if it makes sense, and then they add on.

Let's look together at my piece of writing about _____. I am going to read it aloud to you and I am going to think about whether I can add more to my pictures or my words.

Think aloud as you read your writing, and call attention to places where you might add more details or where you left out something important. Elicit comments and suggestions from students as you consider how to improve your writing

Take a minute to think about the piece you are working on. Think about how you can add more to your pictures or to your words.

Your writing work today is to add more to your writing piece. You can add more to either your pictures or your words. This will make the writing piece better for the reader.

An anchor writing chart encourages student independence.

Top Five Tips for Supporting Independence in Our Readers and Writers

1 Teach your students to be independent before you begin to manage small-group instruction.

In the beginning of the year, it is more important to support your students in the job of becoming independent during reading and writing time than it is to lead small groups. Help students understand the expectations and what they can do when they feel finished so they can learn to work independently.

2 Reward independence.

Stop the class and compliment readers and writers who get materials on their own, who read or write independently for a specific time, and who reach out to help a friend on their own. Give so much love and admiration your students will be enchanted! One compliment we love is the "shooting star": kiss your hand and then make a whooshing noise as you spread your open hand in the direction of the complimented student. Another is the "bouquet." Stop the class and admire a student's actions. Then say: "Let's give _____ a bouquet!" Ask him his favorite flowers and pretend to pull them out of your palm. Then say: "Bloom it for _____!" and float your hand toward the proud recipient of the "bouquet." Compliments and admiration go a long way, especially when you mark those often-unnoticed moments of independence in your young students.

3 Teach your students what to do in all scenarios.

Teach students what they should do when their pencil breaks, when they have to go to the bathroom, if someone is bothering them, if a book rips, if they are out of paper, if they can't think of anything to write about, if, if, if. . . . Spending our time teaching lessons that help our students become independent learners gives us the freedom we need later for small-group teaching.

4 Know your students and what they can do.

You are the best judge of your students and their abilities. Make sure what you are asking them to do during independent time is realistic, doable, and satisfying. Be aware of their age and abilities. Don't try to accomplish everything in one day. Let them have LOTS of success each and every day!

5 Celebrate the small stuff.

It is a big deal when a kindergartner reads for six whole minutes, and a big deal when a second grader is so engrossed in his early chapter book that he can't believe the time is already up. It is a big deal when a first grader has so many topics to write about that she can't choose one since they all feel so important. Celebrate this work, do a silent cheer together or thumbs up, give out reading or writing stamina awards, have a "we are independent" party (make it simple: cookies and juice!). Remember to nurture your learners' pride in their work every day.

You Asked, We Answered

Inspiring independence in our students' work can be the most challenging aspect of our jobs. We know it is not easy. Here are some common questions we are asked.

Q How do I help my students know what to do during independent reading time?

A As teachers we must be very explicit. We cannot take anything for granted. We need to teach our students exactly what it is we want them to do, even if it seems like something tiny. Here are some examples of actual lessons we've taught:

- How students can sit comfortably and productively when they read

- How to take care of books

- What to do when students finish the book in their box or baggie and time is not up (keep on reading)

- How to fill out a reading record

- How to decide when it is time for new books

- How to put books back in their baggie or box

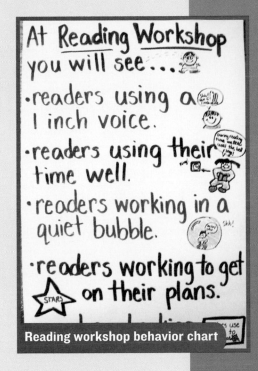

Reading workshop behavior chart

Q How can my students be independent if I do not have enough independent books?

A For our students to be independent they should be engaged with books all the time, and practicing their reading skills at their own reading levels. In addition, students should be able to browse books that are beyond their levels when they are reading on topics of interest to them and below their levels when they are enjoying an easy read to build stamina. But at-level books are essential for each of our students so that they can become stronger readers and work independently. Many of us do not have immediate access to the materials we need, so we have to be creative about how to get appropriate books or reading materials into our students' hands. Here are some ways to get books if you are short on supply:

- Look for education grants or PTA grants online. There are many grants available that give money for resources.

- Read simple poems with your students. Type them up and even laminate them so they are sturdy. Students can illustrate them and put them in their boxes or baggies.

- Share money and resources with your colleagues. If you put together your book allowances from the school, you can order a variety of leveled books from companies such as Wright Group, Rigby, and Scholastic and share them.

- Join AtoZreading.com. On this Web site you can pay a low, one-time fee and print out many leveled books.

Q **How do I help my students use their time well during independent reading and writing?**

A Begin with a management system that celebrates what your children are doing. Give out awards or have a simple celebration with cookies and juice when your students are reading and writing during independent reading time. Also try the following:

- Give awards when they read and write stronger and longer during independent time.

- Give students stamina bookmarks (Resources 5.11 and 5.12) that help students understand your reading and writing expectations.

- Ask parents to get involved. Send home reading and writing plans so there is a consistent home-school connection for our students.

- Make sure expectations are realistic. Start with short periods of independent practice time, and increase time in small increments each day, each week, and each month.

- Make sure students know the expectation for the day; ask them to say it aloud to a partner, check the reading or writing plan chart, or say it out loud to the whole group.

Our Students Can Do It!

If we have high expectations for our students, we can teach them to do anything! Young students want to learn, and they want to feel good about their learning. They savor each moment of their independence. The more time they have to practice independence, the more independent they will become. This independence also gives us more time to meet with small instructional groups or one-on-one with our students. This Great Eight strategy is the cornerstone of differentiated instruction. If we manage our students in ways that allow them to take on independence, we can start grouping them for deep and intensive instructional work without worrying every minute about every other student in the classroom.

Now let's turn to Great Eight strategy #6, Grouping for Success. In this chapter we will help you form reading and writing groups and manage them wisely. Small-group instruction is critical if we want to move our students forward as readers and writers.

Grouping for Success: Effective Small-Group Work

Students come to us with many different needs. One of the most productive forms of instruction is meeting with our students in small groups, which allows us to tailor our instruction in powerful ways. In this chapter we focus on what to teach and how to plan small-group instruction. We will help you feel at ease with grouping by sharing best-practice tips and strategies.

Small-Group Reading Instruction

Now that we have taught our students to work independently, we can begin to meet with small groups for instruction. This instruction occurs during both reading and writing. It provides the opportunity to deliver targeted lessons, teaching to a group of students who have common needs. Groups remain flexible during the year, changing as your students grow as readers and writers.

Assessing Instructional Needs

The fall is a busy time in our school lives. We begin with a new group of excited students. We spend time creating our classroom community and getting to know one another. We must spend valuable time assessing, both formally and informally, to gather information about our students' strengths and challenges. Informal assessments include observations, conversations, and conferences. Formal assessments are conducted two to three times a year to get a baseline reading level. There are many of these assessments on the market. We have found great success with the DRA2 (Developmental Reading Assessment, 2nd ed.) and the Fountas and Pinnell Benchmark Assessment System. (For Fountas and Pinnell levels, see pages 91–94.) Both are comprehensive and assess a student's reading level by looking closely at fluency and comprehension. The data we gather through these assessments helps us make informed decisions about our small groups. If your school does not have a formal assessment in place, take time to meet with your students and make some informed decisions about their reading and writing strengths and challenges.

Configuring Groups

Now that we have our data, we are able to begin to form our groups. This usually occurs in the second month of school. In order for students to get the most of this time, keep group size to six or fewer students. Small group size gives us the ability to tailor our instruction to the group and to support each student. Ideally, our most vulnerable students should be in groups of three or fewer. Groups tend to stay together for approximately one month, at which point we informally reassess and may change the make-up of the groups based on student need.

One way to determine the configuration of groups is to label a box grid with the levels of students or the strategies a class needs. Then, while looking at formal or informal assessment data, write students' names in each box, remembering to keep the group to a maximum of six. This chapter has a variety of planning tools to help you organize your groups in a way that works best for you.

Getting Organized

The best instruction is planned instruction. To make the most of small-group time and alleviate long transitions, here are some tips for managing small groups.

Find a Meeting Place

Once you have determined your small groups, create a place in the room for the groups to meet. This space should be somewhat isolated from other students, who will be working independently. Use a small table, a nice corner of the carpet, or a grouping of student desks.

Post Groups for Students to See

At the end of the day, post the names of students you will be meeting with in groups the next day. This helps students prepare to meet and quickens transition time from one group to the next.

Plan Your Groups in Advance

It is important to know the specific teaching point or reason you are gathering students each day. The goal is to teach the group one explicit point clearly. Start the instruction with a key phrase such as "Today I will teach you...." Knowing your teaching point before beginning your lesson will help make the lesson clear. Also, know the challenges of the book or writing lesson so you can prepare your students for potential tricky spots.

Organize Your Materials

Prior to meeting with groups, make sure everything needed is close at hand. These materials include record-keeping forms, pencils, incentive stickers, teaching notes, chart paper, and books to use in your lesson.

Teaching materials for small groups

Gather Student Materials

If students are reading a new book, it will be provided by the teacher. However, if students are revisiting a book, they will come to the group with this material. For writing lessons, students will need to bring their writing folders or notebooks to the meeting spot. Other materials that should be close by include dry-erase boards, wipe-off markers, magnetic boards, magnetic letters, blank paper, sharpened pencils, and sticky notes.

Be Mindful of Time

If you follow the explicit plans created for your reading or writing group, this will automatically manage time. This is important, because if your plan is to meet with two groups on a certain day, you will need to get to both groups. Keep yourself and your students on topic, using the plans you wrote to stay on task. Take notes in the time between the first and second groups to avoid taking precious minutes away when meeting with students.

Scheduling

Developing a system and a schedule ensures we are able to meet with groups in a timely and regular manner. There are different structures for best organizing our teaching by the month, week, or day.

Monthly Planning

Monthly planning is the key to organizing your reading groups. Revisit group configurations each month to make necessary adjustments as students progress. Some months students stay at about the same level or in the same strategy group; other months you will see big strides. Some instructional groups will remain the same because students are progressing at a relatively uniform rate. Below are some sample planning sheets for organizing groups each month. These can also be found as resources at the back of the book.

Small-Group Reading Instruction—Monthly Planning (Sample 1)
Month: April

Group 1	Group 2	Group 3	Group 4	Group 5
Level: Vulnerable	Level: Vulnerable/Steady	Level: Steady	Level: Steady/Strong	Level: Strong
Students: Sam Cashov Nicole Katrina	Students: Jackson Audomaro Michael Delia Zoe David	Students: Lyle Annie Hugo Annabel Lizzy Louis	Students: Tasha Aleesha Melissa Tyler Sawyer	Students: Jorge Alex Kira Luke

After configuring the groups, the next step is to list instructional needs for the different groupings. Focus your instruction on student needs, not on the book being used. The goal is not to teach a book, but to teach your students: identifying and promoting skills and strategies they can use with any book.

The following sample planning sheets come from a first-grade classroom and show the monthly planning for two of six groups of readers. Note that the teaching points are to be covered throughout the month, not all on one day of instruction.

We use the terms *vulnerable*, *steady*, and *strong* to describe the various levels of reading abilities in our classrooms. Another option is to name your groups by level, based on the formal assessments listed earlier. These terms help when talking to grade-level colleagues about students. Some teachers also identify their groups based on reading level and/or strategy instruction needed.

Small-Group Reading Instruction—Monthly Planning (Sample 2)

Month: April

Group: 1 **Level:** Vulnerable	Group: 5 **Level:** Strong
Children: 1. Sam 2. Cashov 3. Nicole 4. Katrina	**Children:** 1. Jorge 2. Alex 3. Kira 4. Luke
Teaching Points Taking effective picture walks, getting your mouth ready for the beginning sound, checking the picture, using patterns in books, phonics: -ar, -ing, -all	**Teaching Points** Inferring meaning of unknown words based on context clues, retelling, inferring character emotion, marking thinking with sticky notes

The form below shows you how teachers use the Complete 4 as a planning tool for developing teaching points. (See page 144 for more information on the Complete 4.)

Small-Group Reading Instruction—Monthly Planning (Complete 4)

Month: April

Group: 1 **Level:** Vulnerable	
Students: Emily, Wyatt, Sebastian, Yvette, Chris	
Teaching Points	
Process Lessons • taking an effective picture walk	**Genre Lessons** • understanding difference between fiction and nonfiction
Strategy Lessons • decoding unknown words—looking for familiar chunks • identifying a repeated pattern	**Conventions Lessons** • -ar words • how it sounds when you read ending punctuation

Group: 5 **Level:** Strong	
Students: Finnbar, Max, Kira, Vanessa, Cameron	
Teaching Points	
Process Lessons • marking thinking in a book with a sticky note • properly preparing for a partner book talk	**Genre Lessons** • distinguishing between main characters and minor characters
Strategy Lessons • inferring meaning of unknown words (based on context clues) • inferring character emotions—through actions, words, thoughts	**Conventions Lessons** • "r"-controlled vowels

See Resources for reproducible versions of the sample planning forms above: Resource 6.1, Small-Group Reading Instruction—Monthly Planning (Sample 1), page 128; Resource 6.2, Small-Group Reading Instruction—Monthly Planning (Sample 2), page 129; and Resource 6.3, Small-Group Reading Instruction—Monthly Planning (Complete 4), page 130.

Weekly Planning

Now that we have configured our groups and know broad instructional needs for each, we are ready to plan out a week of small-group instruction. Not every group will meet with the same frequency, but each group should get some instruction time every week. Our vulnerable readers in primary grades will need more support from us as they learn how to read. Over time, the amount of instruction for each group will become more equitable as our students become stronger readers.

This first sample schedule shows when each group will be meeting throughout the week. Group 1 is the most vulnerable, and so on. These planning sheets can be found in the Resource section of this book.

Small-Group Reading Instruction—Weekly Planning (Sample 1)

Monday	Tuesday	Wednesday	Thursday	Friday
Group 1	Group 1	Group 1	Group 1	Group 1
Group 2	Group 3	Group 2	Group 3	Group 4

This second sample shows both when each small group will be meeting throughout the week and what teaching point and text will be used.

Small-Group Reading Instruction—Weekly Planning (Sample 2)

	Monday	Tuesday	Wednesday	Thursday	Friday
Group 1	Teaching Point: Taking strong picture walks Text: *Leaves*	Teaching Point: Reading words with the *-an* chunk Text: *Leaves*	Teaching Point: Rereading to make the words sound smooth Texts: *Leaves; Worm Paints*	Teaching Point: Reading pictures for additional story information Text: *Worm Paints*	Teaching Point: Using patterns in text to support reading Text: *Little and Big*
Group 2	Looking for familiar chunks in unfamiliar words Text: *A Bug, a Bear, and a Boy at Home*		Clearing up confusion by rereading Text: *A Bug, a Bear, and a Boy at Home*		
Group 3		Inferring meaning of unknown words based on context clues Text: *Poppleton*		Identifying story elements—main versus minor characters Text: *Poppleton*	
Group 4					Learning about a character through his/her actions and words Text: *Magic Tree House*

In Resources, you'll find reproducible sheets for weekly planning. See page 131 for Resource 6.4, Small-Group Reading Instruction—Weekly Planning (Sample 1), and page 132 for Resource 6.5, Small-Group Reading Instruction—Weekly Planning (Sample 2).

Daily Planning

Let's now plan for each day's instruction, keeping our teaching focused and timely. The first step in creating a daily planning system is to identify the specific teaching point or points for each small group. Record this information. After identifying your instructional focus, select a text that is appropriate for the level of the students and can accommodate your teaching goals. Below are sample planning sheets. These can be found in the Resource pages of this book; choose one that best fits your needs and teaching style.

Small-Group Reading Instruction—Daily Planning (Sample 1)

Level:		Book Title:		Date:	
Teaching Points		**Students**		**Notes**	
Get your mouth ready for beginning sound and check the picture.		Ryan			
		Michaela			
		Jen			
		Christa			
		Shontay			

Small-Group Reading Instruction—Daily Planning (Sample 2)

Date: Friday, Nov. 21

Level: C	Book Title: *Little and Big*
Teaching Points:	**Instructional Notes:**
• Identifying a repeated pattern in a book	• Introduce the name "Dinah"
• Using knowledge of a repeated pattern to anticipate words	• Note that change in the repeated pattern happens early in the text

Students	Observations
Michael	Reads capitalized words with emphasis Does not self-correct errors
Tess	Having difficulty tracking print Self-corrected two errors
Jordan	Easily identified the repeated pattern Used pattern knowledge to read fluently Needs to reread to think about the story
Evie	May be ready to move up a level (*Complete an assessment on Evie) Self-corrected on the page where the pattern changed Was able to retell

Next Steps: Practice more stories at this level with repeated patterns	
Independent Practice to Follow Lesson: Reread the story each day to practice reading fluently	**Teaching Points for Next Lesson:** Identifying repeated patterns in texts Improving fluency and predictions with pattern knowledge

In Resources, you'll find reproducible sheets for daily planning. See page 133 for Resource 6.6, Small-Group Reading Instruction—Daily Planning (Sample 1), and page 134 for Resource 6.7, Small-Group Reading Instruction—Daily Planning (Sample 2).

Small-Group Writing Instruction

Small-group writing instruction is a structure that creates effective and efficient use of time. We meet with groups of writers to teach something explicitly that more than one student needs.

There has been a great movement in the last decade toward more small-group instruction in reading. Now is the time for us to mobilize around small-group writing instruction and really make that teaching matter, too. Grouping children by level, need, and focus gives us the chance to teach more effectively and more efficiently. The Great Eight is all about efficiency, because the big goal is to clarify instructional points and allow teaching and learning to shine through.

Small-group writing instruction

Assessing Instructional Needs

There are three ways to assess students as writers. One is to look closely at individual writing. Another is to listen and observe during whole-group instruction to determine how students are responding to the lesson. The last is to confer with individual students as they write, noticing what they are doing. For more on conferring, see Management Strategy #7.

When looking at individual student writing, take a few minutes to read through their work and list some strengths and weaknesses for each student. Notice patterns—students who need instruction on the same points. Use an organization sheet to list common teaching points. We have made this easy for you by providing lists of skills and strategies students need as writers later in this chapter. See pages 94–96.

Configuring Groups

Keep groups to a maximum of six students. These groups are flexible and will change throughout the year. You will watch your students closely as writers and make ongoing determinations about the composition of groups. At least once a month, do a close review of your groups and change as needed; groups should change—at least in part—every month.

Getting Organized

Have materials ready prior to the lesson, including the following: sticky notes, sharpened pencils, blank paper, stapler, texts to use as examples for specific teaching points, chart paper/wipe-off board/interactive whiteboard, markers or dry erase markers, and laptops, whenever possible.

Scheduling

Meet with your small writing groups regularly. Your vulnerable writers will need more of your support, though all groups should meet at least once each week. This small-group instruction should not take the place of individual conferences, but is yet another crucial way to meet the needs of your students.

Monthly Planning

Plan for monthly, weekly, and daily instruction. Monthly plans have a few different teaching points to focus on at different times during the month. Here are some sample monthly plans for small writing groups.

Small-Group Writing Instruction—Monthly Planning (Sample 1)

Month: April

Group: 1 **Level:** Vulnerable	**Group:** 5 **Level:** Strong
Children: 1. Sam 2. Cashov 3. Nicole 4. Michael 5. Michelle 6. Ryan	**Children:** 1. Jack 2. Alex 3. Kira 4. Dylan 5. Rhyse 6. Leah
Teaching Points Finding writing ideas, oral rehearsal of writing ideas, vowel sounds, "say one more thing" to stretch writing across page	**Teaching Points** Where, when, and how to include internal dialogue, when to use proper nouns versus pronouns, spelling strategy: clapping out multisyllabic words

Small-Group Writing Instruction—Monthly Planning (Complete 4)

Month: April

<table>
<tr><td colspan="2">Group: 1   Level: Vulnerable
Students: Sam, Nicole, Cashov, Michael, Addison</td></tr>
<tr><td colspan="2">Teaching Points</td></tr>
<tr><td>Process Lessons
• finding writing ideas
• oral rehearsal of writing ideas</td><td>Genre Lessons
• writing a label book</td></tr>
<tr><td>Strategy Lessons
• say one more thing</td><td>Conventions Lessons
• long vowel construction: silent e at the end of words
• spacing between words</td></tr>
</table>

<table>
<tr><td colspan="2">Group: 5   Level: Strong
Students: Jack, Alex, Amy, Mahika, José</td></tr>
<tr><td colspan="2">Teaching Points</td></tr>
<tr><td>Process Lessons
• sticking with a topic for a longer period of time</td><td>Genre Lessons
• using features of nonfiction: table of contents and glossary</td></tr>
<tr><td>Strategy Lessons
• using an author as a mentor</td><td>Conventions Lessons
• using varied punctuation for emphasis
• spelling strategy: clapping out a multi-syllabic word</td></tr>
</table>

For reproducible monthly planning forms, see Resource 6.8, Small-Group Writing Instruction—Monthly Planning (Sample 1), on page 135, and Resource 6.9, Small-Group Writing Instruction—Monthly Planning (Complete 4), on page 136.

Weekly Planning

This first sample schedule shows when we meet with small groups and when we confer with individual students.

Small-Group Writing Instruction—Weekly Planning (Sample 1)

Monday	Tuesday	Wednesday	Thursday	Friday
Group 1	Group 1	Individual Conferring	Group 4	Group 1
Group 2	Individual Conferring		Group 3	Individual Conferring

This second sample schedule shows each group and the related teaching points.

Small-Group Writing Instruction—Weekly Planning (Sample 2)

Groups:	1	2	3	4
Teaching Point:	Spelling by stretching	Adding details to pictures	Oral rehearsal before writing	Ending punctuation
Students:	Ty Nia Michael Hugo Grady	Jack Dierdre Peter Zahira	James Tyrone Michelle Timothy	Allison Alisha

For reproducible planning forms, see Resource 6.10, Small-Group Writing Instruction—Weekly Planning (Sample 1), page 137, and Resource 6.11, Small-Group Writing Instruction—Weekly Planning (Sample 2) on page 138.

Daily Planning

Daily writing plans explicitly name teaching points. Here is a sample planning sheet.

Small-Group Writing Instruction—Daily Planning

Date:

Teaching Points:	Teaching Materials:

Students	Observations

Next Steps:	
Independent Practice to Follow Lesson:	Teaching Points for Next Lesson:

See Resource 6.12, Small-Group Writing Instruction—Daily Planning, on page 139, for a reproducible version of the planning form above.

Small-Group Record Keeping

Keeping records or notes of our teaching is essential for tracking progress in our small groups. The sample forms throughout this book and in the Resources section are all useful for planning and keeping records. You can use these in paper form—or better yet, create a file on your laptop and use them that way. Here are two suggestions for developing a record-keeping system that will work for you.

- **Record student names and teaching points prior to meeting.**
  Based on the weekly schedule, record the names of students on planning sheets in advance. Now you are ready to take notes for each student instead of having to write the name down first.

- **Record notes directly after instruction.**
  Set aside a minute or two after your small group to record important notes that will help you support your students as readers and writers.

In Resources, on pages 128–139 and 141–142, you will find sample record-keeping forms.

Organizing Your Records

Access to your records is essential. You can set up binders with monthly tabs to house the daily, weekly, and monthly forms. You can also create virtual folders for keeping track of your records on the computer.

Here is another record-keeping sample that can be used for either reading or writing.

Small-Group Instruction, Reading/Writing

Week of: _____

Monday	Tuesday	Wednesday	Thursday	Friday
Group 1 Notes:	Group 1 Notes:	Group 3 Notes:	Group 1 Notes:	Group 1 Notes:
Group 2 Notes:	Group 2 Notes:	Group 4 Notes:	Group 2 Notes:	Group 3 Notes:

What to Teach in Reading

Teaching points emerge from an understanding of reading levels, a close look at your state standards and formal and informal assessments, and consideration of all four components of what we call the Complete 4: Process, Genre, Strategy, and Conventions.

Students move through typical stages when learning to become proficient readers. In each stage, there are important lessons to help students move from one level to the next. For example, kindergartners learn how to take a picture walk that helps them think about what is happening in a book. In first grade, students learn to self-monitor to see if what they read makes sense. In second grade, readers learn how to monitor for meaning over time as they read chapter books.

On pages 91–94 you'll find lists of teaching points reflecting the Fountas and Pinnell developmental reading levels and our own knowledge of students' reading development. The instruction is organized into four categories—the Complete 4.

Process	Working on fluency, stamina, and independence
Genre	Learning to distinguish among narrative, nonfiction, and poetry
Strategy	Learning strategic reading and writing, practicing reading strategies such as monitoring for meaning and comprehension, honing writing craft to make writing stronger
Conventions	Using grammar and punctuation in real, practical contexts relevant to students' reading and writing experiences

Strong readers and writers show evidence of growth across all four of these critical components. Using these components to plan our small-group instruction makes teaching clearer and more comprehensive. As you have seen throughout this book, we refer to the seminal work of Irene Fountas and Gay Su Pinnell, who have broken new ground in the teaching of reading by establishing levels for books.

Emergent Readers: Levels A, B, C, and the Complete 4

Readers at these levels are matched to simple books with a few words or one line of text per page.

Reading Process	Genre Understandings	Reading Strategies	Conventions

• learning concepts of print:
  • the beginning and end of a word
  • the beginning and end of a sentence
  • the front of the book, the back of the book
  • the difference between words and letters
  • the cover
  • the title and the author
  • how to turn pages
  • which way to open a book
  • where to start reading
  • the difference between the words and the pictures
• activating prior knowledge
• previewing books before reading—cover and title
• previewing books before reading—picture walks
• pointing under the words
• rereading to improve fluency
• increasing stamina by rereading pictures and words
• choosing books to match interest, purpose, and level
	• differentiating between fiction and nonfiction texts
	• recognizing poetic forms and simple poetic qualities such as repetition
	• recognizing that a narrative story has a beginning and end
		• using picture clues to read unknown words
		• getting the mouth ready for the beginning sound
		• monitoring for meaning:
		  • Does it look right? (Using visual cues: Does what I am saying match the letters on the page?)
		  • Does it sound right? (Using syntax: Does what I am saying sound like the English language?)
		  • Does it make sense? (Using meaning: Does what I am saying make sense?)
		• locating known words on a page and using them as anchors
		• relating story to personal experience
		• retelling key ideas of a text
		• using a pattern to predict text
			• understanding left-to-right directionality
			• knowing what one-to-one matching is
			• understanding that ending punctuation signals a pause

Early Readers: Levels D, E, F, and the Complete 4

These readers are matched to books that have two to three lines per page. They have a small bank of sight words and are becoming more skilled at decoding texts.

Reading Process	Genre Understandings	Reading Strategies	Conventions
• previewing books before reading—cover and title • previewing books before reading—picture walk • rereading to improve fluency • rereading to improve comprehension • increasing reading stamina by rereading a familiar book • increasing stamina by reading a new book for a longer period of time	• identifying differences between fiction and nonfiction texts • recognizing basic poetic qualities such as white space and repetition • demonstrating awareness of beginning, middle, and end in a story • recognizing characters in stories and developing some sense of setting	• self-correcting • monitoring for meaning: Does it look right? Sound right? Make sense? • using known words and parts of words to figure out unknown words • activating prior knowledge to help with comprehension • retelling through recall of important story elements or key facts • relating story to personal experience • predicting story events before and during reading • identifying patterns in texts and understanding how patterns change • pointing at words only when experiencing difficulty • rereading when something does not make sense	• using knowledge of letter sounds to decode words • recognizing common "chunks" in words • reading with attention to punctuation • identifying suffixes (-ed, -es, -ing)

An interactive chart supports readers as they practice reading strategies. Students are given their own reading toolbox as a reminder to try the following strategies when they come to a tricky spot:

- Look at the word.
- Look at the picture.
- Get your mouth ready for the beginning sound.
- Ask yourself, "Does it look right? Does it sound right? Does it make sense?"

See also Resource 6.13, Reading Toolbox Strategies, page 140.

Transitional Readers: Levels G, H, I, and the Complete 4

These readers are beginning to integrate meaning, structure, and visual cues to read more fluently. The books range from a few sentences to a few paragraphs on each page.

Reading Process	Genre Understandings	Reading Strategies	Conventions
• rereading to improve fluency • rereading to improve comprehension • choosing level, uphill, and downhill books • increasing reading stamina by reading for longer periods of time • talking to a partner to deepen comprehension	• reading a variety of genres • recognizing that genre understanding supports deeper comprehension • identifying and using nonfiction text features such as table of contents, headings, and captions • recognizing when a fiction story becomes unclear or confusing • predicting story events before and during reading • questioning the events in a story	• monitoring for meaning • using context cues to find the meaning of a new word • questioning actions in a story • integrating structural and visual cues • self-correcting • sustaining comprehension in a chapter book after putting it down and picking it up the next day • relating a story to personal experiences or another text • creating mental images to support comprehension • retelling the important parts of a book • inferring the meaning of unknown words • recognizing and reading compound words • subvocalizing when reading	• understanding how conventions guide fluency and how fluent reading sounds • knowing how punctuation guides intonation • using punctuation to understand who is talking

Transitional Readers: Levels J, K, and the Complete 4

At this level, readers are matched to texts that are much longer and more complex; many have discovered the joys of beginning chapter books and series. Students are developing higher-level thinking skills.

Reading Process	Genre Understandings	Reading Strategies	Conventions
• reading silently • building stamina through reading and rereading books in various genres and levels	• identifying story elements • having a balanced reading diet—books from different genres • reading and understanding chapter books • skimming nonfiction books for information • making connections to various characters • understanding plot • recognizing new poetry forms • inferring from images in poems	• integrating three cueing systems (visual elements, syntax, meaning) to read unknown words • understanding the main idea of the story • making predictions • inferring meaning of unknown words • inferring character emotions	• decoding in chunks rather than letter by letter • using punctuation to read accurately and fluently

Extended Readers: Levels L, M, N, and the Complete 4

At this level, books are longer with smaller print. There are few pictures and the books require more background knowledge for comprehension.

Reading Process	Genre Understandings	Reading Strategies	Conventions
• reading silently • building stamina through reading and rereading books in various genres and levels • jotting notes in preparation for book conversations • activating prior knowledge • using texts as references • becoming a critical reader	• identifying story elements with ease, helping to support comprehension • having a balanced reading diet—books from different genres • reading and understanding chapter books • reading nonfiction texts and making connections across the different books • identifying similes and metaphors in poetry	• integrating three cueing systems (visual elements, syntax, meaning) to read unknown words • understanding main idea of the story • making predictions • inferring meaning of unknown words • inferring character emotions • searching for and interpreting information in texts	• using word parts to solve new words • reading with expression using punctuation

For more information on other strategies to teach at different levels, see Fountas and Pinnell's *The Continuum of Literacy Learning, K–2* (Heinemann, 2007).

What to Teach in Writing

In much the same way readers grow across developmental phases—emergent, early, transitional, extended, and fluent—so writers grow, developing increasingly sophisticated strategies to help them control and use writing to serve a range of needs and interests across genre and function. Young children develop confidence as writers when they're able to write about events, ideas, and learning discoveries across the curriculum that hold personal meaning.

Emergent Writers

These writers have not had much experience writing and are new to the idea of communicating ideas through pictures and words. Sound-symbol correspondence is just beginning.

Writing Process	Genre Understandings	Writing Strategies	Conventions
• knowing why writers write and what the purpose for their writing will be • reviewing work and then adding more (to picture and/or text) • building stamina: increasing time spent in sustained writing/drawing as well as length of what is written or drawn • selecting appropriate materials (including types of paper)	• writing on a beloved topic in various genres • using story language to write/tell a story • labeling simple captions for a nonfiction piece • using some rhythm and/or repetition for poetry	• finding a writing idea • communicating meaning through pictures • talking as rehearsal for writing • sketching a writing idea • adding more to pictures and words • using all story elements to tell a story • labeling pictures	• forming letters appropriately • using proper directionality • spacing between words • using knowledge of the alphabet to spell new words • using an alphabet chart to add print and improve spelling

Early Writers

These writers are communicating through pictures and some words. Knowledge of sound-symbol correspondence is growing.

Writing Process	Genre Understandings	Writing Strategies	Conventions
• stretching writing/ drawing across numerous pages • rereading to add on • rereading to revise • using prewriting tools to organize ideas/ information • staying with one piece of writing for a period of time	• finding writing ideas • writing on a beloved topic in various genres • writing with a beginning, middle, and end • showing basic research for a nonfiction wondering • demonstrating some understanding of poetic rhythm and repetition	• talking as rehearsal for writing • adding details to pictures and words to strengthen the story • using the word wall to spell high-frequency words correctly • visualizing story to add details to writing • using prior knowledge about a topic to add more to a story	• capitalizing the beginning of sentences • using ending punctuation • spacing between words • using capital letters for names • using the word wall as a spelling resource • spelling by stretching the sounds in words

Transitional Writers

These writers are able to write multiple sentences. Knowledge of various genres is emerging.

Writing Process	Genre Understandings	Writing Strategies	Conventions
• stretching writing across numerous pages • rereading to add on • rereading to revise • using prewriting tools to organize ideas/ information • sticking with one piece of writing for a period of time	• stating a big idea and supporting it • writing a story with a problem and a solution • proving an idea with facts • experimenting with basic forms of poetry	• creating a story plan using plan sheets with pictures and words • telling a story in sequence to prepare for writing • replicating craft techniques from mentor texts in own writing • writing about characters in detail • writing about setting in detail • using nonfiction text features in nonfiction writing	• using ending punctuation • using capitalization appropriately • organizing topics into chunks/paragraphs • writing with subject-verb agreement • clapping out multi-syllabic words to improve spelling • using the word wall and other print in the room to spell challenging words • using knowledge of spelling patterns to spell challenging words

Writing charts

Extended Writers

These writers can easily write multiple sentences. They are spelling some common patterns and high-frequency words correctly. These writers rely less on pictures for rehearsal and communicating information and more on words.

Writing Process	Genre Understandings	Writing Strategies	Conventions
• rereading to add details • rereading to revise • rereading to fix grammar and spelling • writing a strong lead • writing a satisfying ending	• writing in response to reading • summarizing main ideas, orally and in writing • writing using all story elements (characters, problem, solution, setting, time) • writing to demonstrate understanding of an idea and supporting it with facts • writing to express an opinion in writing • writing to visualize an image in a poem	• including sensory details • using multiple sources for nonfiction writing • creating visual images in writing • incorporating craft elements into leads and endings • using comprehension strategies to monitor own writing	• writing with consistent verb tense • using proper names and pronouns • using internal punctuation (ellipses, quotation marks, commas) • utilizing spelling resources effectively for unknown words • applying spelling strategies effectively for unknown words

Two Spelling Strategies for Extended Writers

• **Clap It Out:** Clap out a multisyllabic word and spell one chunk at a time.

• **Try Three:** Write a word three times in the margin of the paper, and choose the spelling that looks correct.

Fluent Writers

These are strong, independent writers who are able to convey their message clearly and accurately. They enjoy writing and are beginning to experiment with many different types of writing.

Writing Process	Genre Understandings	Writing Strategies	Conventions
• creating writing goals (based on process, genre, strategy, or conventions) • building organizational skills and individual responsibility • using mentor texts for inspiration • preplanning writing • sticking with a writing piece for an extended period of time • communicating with others through writing • using partnerships/ groups to explore and develop writing ideas • adding thoughts and feelings to narrative scenes	• writing a simple play • writing a narrative with a theme • writing expository paragraphs with topic sentence and some factual details • writing poems with more than a literal message	• writing with vivid, attention-getting language • using metaphor to extend levels of meaning • structuring multiple paragraphs in a logical order • using effective transitions • using text features and graphic aids for clarification	• using varied sentence structure • using paragraphs to organize topics • using pausing punctuation • using punctuation to influence fluency and meaning (bold words, ellipses, parentheses) • using varied verbs (action, state-of-being, helping) • using adjectives and adverbs • adding meaningful dialogue • using spelling resources effectively

Top Five Tips for Small-Group Instruction

1 Assess your students.

The makeup of your small groups is based on ongoing assessment of students. Close observation, running records, dialogue with your students, and the regular administration of strong assessment tools will provide information about students' strengths, challenges, and commonalities.

2 Plan your instruction.

Plan your teaching prior to engaging with your small groups. Have the books ready for a small reading group and any anchor texts ready for a small writing group. Have your explicit teaching point on your planning sheet.

3 Take notes.

Record notes on each student after meeting with small groups. This will help you see how students have grown as readers and writers and decide on next steps and lessons.

4 Flexibility is key.

Some of your students are going to fly forward. Others will, for various reasons, come up against bumps in the road and need some extra-special care. The flexibility of groupings means you can honor and tune in to each student's needs.

5 Get support.

Your colleagues can be very helpful to you in planning for small groups. Find one colleague to meet with to review assessment notes, concerns, or questions to help make your small-group planning successful. Take one common prep period a week to share your notes on students with your colleagues. Let them give you feedback, and do the same for them.

Small-group plan sheet

Take notes while working with your students.

You Asked, We Answered

Q **The make-up of my small groups tends to stay consistent all year. Am I doing something wrong?**

A Some of our students will stay in the same "category" for learning all year. Some of our strong readers will be with other strong readers all year and some of our vulnerable writers will be in small groups for vulnerable students all year. However, you should have at least a third of your students moving from group to group throughout the year. Make sure that you are paying close attention to student needs and your record keeping in small groups and conferences. Use these notes to place students with peers with similar instructional needs.

Q **How often should I be meeting with my students in small groups?**

A Our most vulnerable readers and writers need the most support in small-group instruction. Meet with these students four to five times a week. Meet with your steady students two to three times a week and your strong students one to two times a week—*all* your students need some small-group time.

Your students will quickly come to understand the flow of this schedule. They love to meet with you, and a side benefit to small-group instruction is the opportunity they get to meet and work with one another in very different ways than they do in a whole-class setting. In our many conversations and interviews with students, we have been struck by how much students appreciate the small-group time, not just for their time with you, but also to work side by side with other children. If they are grouped well, our students come to trust these structures as extremely supportive to their needs and a sanctuary for their own learning and growth.

The best management strategies are those that feel so much a part of what you do that they become nearly invisible. This chapter's Great Eight strategy for coordinating small groups will become that way, too, even though when you first start managing them, it may feel like spinning plates! We promise, however, that as you practice meeting with small groups, and as you implement the other Great Eight strategies, your teaching will feel a lot less like juggling and a lot more like what you really want it to be.

No More Juggling!

Running small groups take practice. If one day feels bumpy, don't give up. Your students will thrive if their needs are met and they can find commonalities in one another's growth steps.

We now turn to Great Eight Strategy #7, one that complements #6 in addressing the needs of each individual. Through these strategies, we are aiming for the ultimate differentiated classroom: one in which every student is thriving and growing toward his or her potential. This strategy will help you organize your teaching so that you can hit the mark with each of your students.

Differentiating Instruction: How to Reach All Learners

This Great Eight strategy is a magical ingredient. What we find is that in classrooms where students are being seen one-on-one on a regular basis, the management of the entire class immediately improves. Why? This is because it is human nature to crave that one-on-one. To be known. To be understood. And in the context of a classroom, it is sometimes difficult to be known or to be understood. With structures in place for that one-on-one, instantly your whole-group management will feel easier.

Individual Instruction: The One-on-One Reading and Writing Conference

The word *confer* means to consult together, carry on a conversation, and express an opinion. Conferring is a wonderful opportunity to talk with students about their reading and writing work, to discover what is going well, to coach them through what is feeling hard, and to forge a deep and lasting connection with students. Conferring is often just the opportunity students need to get over a particular challenge, the support they need to surge ahead in their learning.

Conferring Strategies

Like small-group instruction, conferring requires some planning and note taking. Here are some strategies to prepare for the conference.

Strategy One: Create a class check-in.

This schedule shows what and how much support students received during a week's time, making it easy to see who else needs support.

Class Check-In Sheet

Week of: 1/19		
Name	Small Group	Conference
Taylor	XX	
Patty	X	X
Rhyse		
Dylan	XXX	
Oscar	XXX	

Strategy Two: Have your recording system ready.

Through our records we chart growth, determine next steps, and hold students accountable to our teaching. Our conference records influence both our small-group and whole-class instruction. Recording our instruction and making the time to reflect on our records result in powerful teaching. Sample record-keeping forms can be found throughout the chapter and in the Resource section of this book.

Strategy Three: Bring children's literature with you to the conference.

Demonstration is an essential component in teaching. Carrying a few favorite read-alouds when conferring gives us the ability to demonstrate a reading or writing lesson in a familiar text.

Strategy Four: Develop a "Do Not Disturb" signal.

Our conferring time is sacred. Here are ways to signal that you are working one-on-one with a student and cannot be disturbed unless it is an emergency.

- Place a mini stop sign or mini traffic cone on the desk or table where you are conferring.
- Wear a conferring lei.
- Wear a conferring crown.
- Meet at a designated "Do Not Disturb" conferring table.
- Hold a conferring wand.

Creating a Schedule That Works

Students should be seen in a reading conference at least every other week. In writing, this will occur more often, as the balance of small-group instruction can be a little easier. Below are two scheduling options: an integrated schedule, and separate conferring and small-group instruction times in the same day.

Integrated Schedule

Creating an integrated schedule is one way to balance small-group instruction and conferences. Each week, certain days are designated for small-group instruction and others for conferring. Using this model, each day will consist of two to three small groups or five students in conferences.

Monday	Tuesday	Wednesday	Thursday	Friday
Small Groups Groups 1, 2	Small Groups Groups 1, 2, 3	Conferences Anna, AJ, Elle, Andrew, Kevin	Small Groups Groups 1, 4	Conferences Jonathon, Cori, Alesha, Sarah, Luis

Separate Conferring and Small-Group Instruction Time

Some primary classrooms have a literacy center or a partner reading time regularly scheduled into the day. In this case, twice a week during this time, meet with individual students for conferences. One of the literacy centers can be a conferring table, or a reading conference "train," where students bring their independent reading boxes or baggies to a table and rotate to meet with you. The students are all at a similar reading level, and they read independently while their classmates confer with the teacher. Inevitably, they overhear others' conferences, which is a desired side effect of the conferring table. The instruction for one student may be beneficial for others at that level. With this schedule, students will be seen every other week in a reading conference. During independent reading time, continue to pull small groups.

Students on the conference train read independently while others confer with the teacher.

Monday	Tuesday	Wednesday	Thursday	Friday
Partner Reading Time or Literacy Centers: Conference Group A	Partner Reading Time or Literacy Centers	Partner Reading Time or Literacy Centers: Conference Group B	Partner Reading Time or Literacy Centers	Partner Reading Time or Literacy Centers
Independent Reading Time: Small Groups 1 and 2	Independent Reading Time: Small Groups 1 and 3	Independent Reading Time: Small Groups 2 and 4	Independent Reading Time: Small Groups 1 and 5	Independent Reading Time: Small Groups 3 and 6

The next week's cycle will be for conference groups C and D.

Key Components of a Conference

The purpose of a conference is not simply to judge how well a student reads his book or writes his narrative, but to give him new tools and understandings so he can read and write more successfully. The way to do this is through a predictable conference structure. We plan **before**, teach **during**, and reflect and take notes **after** the conference.

Before the Conference

The day or week before the conference, we plan with whom we will meet. The day before the meeting, review past conference notes, writing folders or notebooks, and/or book baggies and boxes. Draw on your knowledge about your students as readers and writers. Enter into the conference with possible teaching ideas for the student, even before engaging in conversation with him or her.

During the Conference

We follow a consistent framework inside the conference. We mix in the following elements and take notes during the meeting. (See Conference Notes, Resource 7.1, page 141.)

Assess and compliment.

Every conference begins with a conversation about the students' reading or writing work.
It is a balance of what you already know about this student and what is happening on this day. We use information from this conversation to inform our instruction.

Engage your student in a brief and focused discussion about his reading or writing work. What feels good about the work? What feels hard? How is he implementing the instruction from the whole-class lesson? Assess both instructional needs and areas of growth at this point of the conference. Give each student an explicit and authentic compliment.

Teach.

After discussing the reading or writing work in which your students are engaged, decide on one explicit teaching point. Use the same phrase from whole-class and small-group instruction, "Today I'm going to teach you. . ." to make your teaching clear. After stating your teaching point, demonstrate what it is you want your student to do. Ask the student to try what you have just taught, and coach as necessary.

Try.

Ask your students to try what you have just taught, right there on the page or screen, and coach as needed.

Clarify.

At the end of the conference, clearly summarize the teaching point and what you want the student to work on going forward: "Today you learned that if you stop partway through a book to work on a tricky word, you go back and reread the sentence to understand what is happening on that page. As you continue reading independently, I want you to practice rereading sentences if you stop partway through to work on a tricky word. When you practice this smart reading work, mark one sentence with a sticky note so you can share it." This clarifying statement summarizes what was taught and explicitly explains how the student is to continue practicing this work.

After the Conference

Immediately after the conference, jot down information you have learned about your students. It is best to record this information before beginning a new conference, while the information is fresh in your mind. (See Post-Conference Notes, Resource 7.2, page 142.) There are three key pieces of information to record.

The Compliment

Record what you noticed the student doing well as evidence of achievement.

The Teaching Point

State the teaching point briefly so you can check back or continue this teaching in future conferences.

Future Lessons

Since there are multiple possible teaching points in a single conference, and you have chosen only one, record the others for future individual instruction, a small group, or the whole class, if you notice patterns.

Record-Keeping Systems for Conference Notes

A record-keeping system is essential to organizing and using information gathered in conferences. A good system allows you to see your students as individuals and the class as a whole. Reviewing conference notes on one student allows you to track growth and hold students accountable to teaching. Reviewing conference notes across a group of students enables you to see patterns of instructional needs to plan small-group or whole-class instruction.

Teacher's conference notes

Resource 7.3: Keep this helpful resource accessible, and use it as a guide for effective conferring. (See Resources, page 143.)

Recording Systems

Choose one of the options below for recording notes on planning sheets and revise to meet your students' needs—or devise your own unique system.

Whole-Class Recording Sheets

These sheets are divided into 10–15 boxes with individual names in each box. This way, notes about the entire class can be recorded on two sheets of paper. These recording sheets can be kept on a clipboard or in your laptop and later put into a binder (virtual or actual) by month.

Student: Tyrone Date:	Student: Michael Date:	Student: Eva Date:	Student: Chandra Date:
Student: Leo Date:	Student: Rachel Date:	Student: Deundre Date:	Student: Clara Date:

Individual Recording Sheets

Another way to keep notes is to have a recording sheet for each student, with an additional whole-class check-off sheet to keep track of the students with whom you have met. This way, the notes for each student are on one page, and you can look across your notes for the next individual teaching point.

Student: _____

Date:	Title of Book/Writing:
Observations and Compliment	
Teaching Point	
Future Teaching	

For reproducible recording sheets, see Resources 7.1 and 7.2.

Sticky Notes and Stickers

Using sticky notes or stickers is another useful way to keep conference notes. Divide the binder/notebook into sections using dividers, one for each student in the class. Mailing labels (2" x 4") or sticky notes marked with individual student names are used to record the individual's conference notes. Once all labels are completed (all students have received a conference), look across the notes to plan for small-group and whole group instruction. Finally, individual notes are peeled off and filed behind students' tabs.

To see your class as a whole, lay out both pages of mailing labels or sticky notes to scan across the class. To see your students as individuals, turn to student tabs and review past conference notes. The benefit of this system is a well-organized binder where individual students are easy to track.

> In order to get a sense of your class, lay out both pages of conference notes. Flip through the pages to track different students. Student names will be in the same location on each recording sheet so you will look at that particular box in past weeks. Benefits of this system: The clipboard is easy to carry around. It is a one-step record-keeping process.

Notebooks

Individual notebooks can also be used to record conference notes. The notebooks should be small in size and light—like the "blue books" used for test-taking in upper elementary grades. Notebooks are stored in the students' writing folders and in their reading boxes or baggies. Each time you meet with a student, use the notebook to record the date, teaching point, and notes. To look at instructional needs across the class, use a whole-class recording form as well.

Technology

Technology provides another way to take notes easily. If you have a laptop, carry it with you to conferences and adapt the ideas above for the screen.

Top Five Tips for Conferring With Students

1 Compliment your students.

In each conference, compliment the student. An explicit compliment is in itself a teaching point, as it tells students to continue something they are doing well in their reading or writing work. "I like the way you went back and reread the sentence after working on the word *school*. When you reread, it helps you better understand what is happening in your book. Good work!" Never underestimate the power of positive language. It is undeniably powerful and likely to stick long beyond the conference.

2 Teach students what to do when you're busy conferring.

Discuss and chart with the class what to do when their pencil breaks, they have to go to the bathroom, they are thirsty, their book rips, someone is bothering them, and so on. Establish a list of what to do when these and other situations occur, so students can be successful without interrupting you.

3 Create an "I need you" or "parking lot" board.

Students can put their name on a sticky note, label it *I need you* or *parking lot* (to address later), and place it on the board when you are in a conference. When you are available, you can assist these students. This validates that their needs matter, but reminds them that they need to wait until you are finished. Often, by the time you get back to them they already will have solved the problem.

4 Teach students when it is okay to interrupt.

Explain to students explicitly when it is okay to interrupt, which is usually only if there is an emergency. An emergency is if someone is hurt, if there is a fire, if someone is sick, or if there truly is another urgent situation unfolding that requires your immediate attention. It may happen that a student really needs something and must interrupt. But once students know what to do in other cases and understand that there are ways to get your feedback later, they won't need to interrupt.

5 Be prepared.

We cannot stress enough the importance of being prepared. We maximize our time with students when we have an idea of where they are as writers or what they are reading. Look through past teaching notes, student independent books, and writing folders prior to meeting with your students.

You Asked, We Answered

Here are some common questions about one-on-one instruction and conferring.

Q **How often do I need to confer with my readers and writers?**

A Conferring with your readers and writers gives you valuable information about how effectively your students are able to apply previous instruction *independently*. Information you gain in conferences informs how you configure your small groups for instruction as you learn about each student's strengths and weaknesses. Meet with your students in individual conferences at least twice a month. If you are able to work out a schedule that enables you to meet with greater frequency, that's great! All students should receive instruction in a small group *or* a conference two to three times a week.

Q **My conferences end up taking so long—at least 15 minutes. What can I do to keep them short?**

A Keep your conferences to 5–8 minutes, using the Reading and Writing Conference Quick Reference (Resource 7.3, page 143) to structure them. Carry familiar texts with you to the conference to demonstrate one teaching point. Most important, plan ahead—read students' writing in advance of the conference and review your own notes.

Q **When is the best time to record my conference notes?**

A At the conclusion of a conference, jot your notes down right away, before moving on to another student. Record the compliment, teaching point, and future lessons for each conference (see Resource 7.2, page 142) while they are still fresh in your mind; this should take only a minute or two.

From One-to-One to the Power of the Whole

To learn about students as individual readers and writers, nothing is more powerful then conferring. To confer—or converse—allows us to get to know our students as people and guide them in ways we never could have without this time. As we think of ways to support our students, we remember that the conference is the key to differentiated instruction: the kind of teaching that really meets the needs of every single child in our classroom. This is no easy task, but meeting one-on-one with our students is the very best way to honor the small steps of one student as well as the giant steps of another.

In this final section, we share with you classroom-tested strategies for bringing all those voices together so that your community is strong and effective. The ultimate management strategy is to create a place where all students feel heard and all students are celebrated.

Building Community: Celebrating Readers and Writers

We have seen many classrooms where there are lots of pieces in place, but one secret, fabulous ingredient is missing. That ingredient is celebration. We see teachers wait to celebrate until the end of the year, until a child does well on a test, until the child actually masters the art of reading. But why wait? Celebration is the ultimate management strategy, because it impacts every other management strategy in the Great Eight. It is the core ingredient that infuses the entire life of the classroom with joy, with hope, with faith, and with optimism.

Compliment your students.

Think of your own life... the time someone said something to you that gave you hope or a sense of the uniqueness of who you are. When someone celebrates your accomplishment, small as it may seem, it gives you the courage to continue. When celebration is missing, the classroom never feels as strong or as secure.

Here is a top ten list for how to use celebration as the key management strategy: the key that will build community, sustain each individual student, and help achieve the kinds of outcomes for your readers and writers that you had only dreamed of.

Give students an opportunity to celebrate.

1 Make a list called "Admirations," and keep it in your laptop or in a folder on your desk.

Every day, be sure you find something to admire in five of your students. By Friday, each student has heard from you at least once about something specific in his or her growth as a reader or writer. Be as specific as you can be. "Bobby, I so loved how you worked with your partner." "Sarah, I really liked how you got comfortable quickly in your reading spot this week." Read through the Admirations each week. You will also learn about your students by reflecting on what you notice about them.

2 Give each student a reading and writing compliment on an index card or a sticky note at least once a week.

Find something lovely to say. It doesn't have to be something big. Say something like "I really loved how you used capital letters in your writing this week." Or: "I was so happy to see you helping your writing partner." Or: "The poem you wrote made me smile."

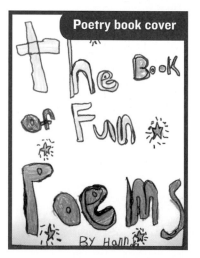
Poetry book cover

3 Have a poetry museum or a poetry party on Fridays.

Name students' little musings "poetry" and make a big fuss over them. Primary students speak in poetry! Record their wonderful observations and call it poetry. Let them play with words and have fun putting their words to music or chants or beats. Display their writing every Friday as if it is the most precious thing in the world.

4 Have a basket for students' own writing.

When students finish their work, or write something on their own, put the writing in the basket for other students to see. Keep the basket in the classroom library so students come to value their own writing as much as they would anyone else's. If it's available, students can select their friends' writing to read during independent reading time, too, which is a huge compliment to the author.

Class nonfiction books

Shared class books

Individual published books

5 Don't underestimate bulletin boards.

Over the years, as literacy education has become more process oriented, we have diminished the role bulletin boards can play in helping children feel great about their work. Take time to feature student work in both reading and writing in beautiful ways on bulletin boards both inside and outside your classroom. Label the bulletin boards with language that truly celebrates growth in reading and writing. "See how we find writing ideas!" "Look at what Classroom K1 is reading this week!" "Student writers share tips on how to write a story!" Your students will feel proud and the school hallways will come alive with the glory of authentic student work, neatly displayed and in celebration of process.

"Quiet bubble" bulletin board

Ms. Smith's Kindergarten Students Are Terrific At

Sitting In A Quiet Bubble For Independent Reading!!!

Students share their writing with classmates.

Infuse the classroom with joy and celebration.

6 **Celebrate your students as readers by honoring each small step.**

"I appreciate how you sat knee-to-knee today." "I appreciate how you read in a one-inch voice so that others could read quietly." Don't let anything small escape your attention. These are teachable moments, and your entire class will be noticing what you choose to compliment and will want to do the same.

7 **Give each child a "shooting star" at least one day during the week for working independently (even if it's for only two minutes!).**

The "shooting star" is a kiss to your palm and then a waving out of your hand toward your recipient, with a *whooshing* sound. The children will love it!

8 **Give personal "thumbs up" signs to each student who turns and talks successfully, adds on to what someone else says, offers an opinion, and generally is deeply engaged in the whole-class instruction.**

Let your students know you will always give a "thumbs up" when you notice something really wonderful, and when you don't want to interrupt to say something about it. Each child will appreciate those little "thumbs up" moments so much. Make sure you are thoughtful about how you spread the "wealth," and share the positive gesture with all children in your room each week.

Thumbs up! Students celebrate one another.

9 Turn the negatives into positives.

When you see a child's attention seem to wander, stop yourself before you immediately try to "correct" the behavior. Instead, ask yourself: "How could I reframe this for both me and the child?" So, for example, when you see a child daydreaming, you could say: "Class, look at Mike! He is such a writer at work! He is gazing out the window to generate his writing ideas. He is dreaming new ideas for the day's work. I am excited to see what he will come up with today." Say it genuinely and with true care so that Mike and everyone in the class feels your natural enthusiasm and your optimism that Mike is trying to do the right thing.

10 Take time to manage your own stress, and create a lifestyle and environment for yourself that will reflect positively on your students.

Management is not only about what you can do for children. It's what you can do for yourself. The Great Eight is a toolkit for YOU, so that you can put all the pieces in place that will most support your teaching. The calm, happy, centered you is going to be the best teacher you can be.

As we come to the final moments of this book journey together, remember to celebrate your own growth, your own professional journeys. The way we manage our celebrations reflects how we live our lives. Let each day in the classroom be a celebration of learning, of childhood, and of community for you and for your students.

Be positive with your students.

Set a peaceful, happy tone.

Classroom Environment Checklist

Library

The classroom library has the following:

- [ ] no more than 15 books in a basket, with covers facing forward so they are easy to browse
- [ ] fiction baskets with books clearly labeled and sorted by categories and author (e.g., school, feelings, animals, pets, favorite read-alouds, holidays, seasons, series such as Henry and Mudge and Poppleton, alphabet, math and counting, hello readers, wordless books, folktales, fairy tales, etc.)
- [ ] nonfiction baskets with books clearly labeled by topic or type (e.g., how to, cooking, land animals, ocean animals, insects, food, reference books, space, magazines, etc.)
- [ ] an identification system with stickers to identify where books go (e.g., alphabet books all have a red heart sticker and the label on the basket does as well)
- [ ] baskets of leveled books (20–30% of library)
- [ ] all books within student reach
- [ ] a basket of student-written and class-published books
- [ ] a shelf or basket for read-alouds
- [ ] a place to store big books
- [ ] a laptop with access to online books (e.g., realebooks.com)

Meeting Area

The meeting area has the following:

- [ ] easel with chart paper and/or wipe-off board
- [ ] teacher materials: markers, sticky notes, and tape
- [ ] rug area
- [ ] clipboard with lesson plan
- [ ] place for read-alouds
- [ ] big book holder
- [ ] calendar area
- [ ] schedule that is clear and easy for students to follow
- [ ] board or wall space for displaying lists of students who have daily conferences and guided reading
- [ ] board or wall space where partnerships are listed
- [ ] chart showing center assignments
- [ ] interactive whiteboard or other technology that supports whole-class instruction

Tabletops

Tabletops have the following, as needed:

- [ ] book baskets for browsing
- [ ] materials for students (caddy with pencils, erasers, crayons, colored pencils, scissors, glue sticks, etc.), neatly organized
- [ ] student name tags on tables and/or chairs

Student Materials

Student materials are organized in a variety of ways:

- [ ] large, resealable plastic bags for student independent books (in bins by table)
- [ ] writing folders personalized by students organized in caddies by table with individual word walls inside
- [ ] bins with paper for writing
- [ ] bins or a place for tape, staplers, and other needs for writers
- [ ] bins or other storage for various shared materials

Small-Group Instruction

The area for small-group instruction includes the following:

- [ ] clipboard or notebook with guided reading plans
- [ ] clipboard or notebook for conferring notes
- [ ] bin for guided reading books
- [ ] wipe-off boards
- [ ] dry-erase markers
- [ ] guided books ready to use for day's lesson
- [ ] pencils
- [ ] magnetic letters or tiles

Wall Space

Classroom walls display the following:

- [ ] reading and writing anchor charts that are easy to see and pertain to units of study in progress
- [ ] a word wall that is usable for students, with either hook-and-loop fasteners, so students can take the words off and bring them to their seats, or large, clear print in a place where all students can see the words
- [ ] student work
- [ ] signs made by students
- [ ] clear environmental print (desk, window, door, etc.)

Walls outside the classroom display the following:

- [ ] colorful work by students, showing clear evidence of reading and writing work in the classroom, labeled by the teacher

Center Space

The classroom has the following student work areas:

- [ ] listening center that is easily accessible to students and well marked so they know how to use it
- [ ] block area with clear photos to show where blocks are returned
- [ ] storage space for big books that students can access
- [ ] storage place for materials for centers, organized in bins that are clearly labeled (word work magnets, art materials, etc.)

Teacher Professional Space

A space for teacher materials includes the following:

- [ ] a bin or shelf for teacher's read-alouds for units of study
- [ ] a plan book and note-taking tools or binder
- [ ] professional books
- [ ] binders with units of study and supplemental materials
- [ ] pens, pencils, tape, and other teacher materials, clearly labeled
- [ ] your own computer for record-keeping and unit planning

Community Spaces

There are places in the room for the following:

- [ ] mailboxes (hanging shoe bags or a mailbox for each student)
- [ ] basket for finished work
- [ ] basket for notes
- [ ] art materials

Read-Alouds for the Beginning of the Year

Title of Book	Author	Genre
Lucky Pennies and Hot Chocolate	Carol D. Shields	Fiction
The Teeny Tiny Teacher	Stephanie Calmenson	Fiction
Chameleons Are Cool	Martin Jenkins	Nonfiction
T-Rex	Vivian French	Nonfiction
Surprising Sharks	Nicola Davies	Nonfiction
The Usborne First Encyclopedia series	Various authors	Nonfiction
The Great Gracie Chase: Stop That Dog!	Cynthia Rylant	Fiction
Night in the Country	Cynthia Rylant	Fiction
Tough Boris	Mem Fox	Fiction
Wilfrid Gordon McDonald Partridge	Mem Fox	Fiction
Whoever You Are	Mem Fox	Fiction
Alphabet Mystery	Audrey Wood	Fiction
Kitten's First Full Moon	Kevin Henkes	Fiction
When I Was Five	Arthur Howard	Fiction
Reading Makes You Feel Good	Todd Parr	Fiction
Sunflower House	Eve Bunting	Fiction
My Visit to the Aquarium	Aliki	Nonfiction
"Let's Get a Pup!" Said Kate	Bob Graham	Fiction
Robots	Clive Gifford	Nonfiction
Wolf!	Becky Bloom	Fiction
The Night I Followed the Dog	Nina Laden	Fiction
Not Norman: A Goldfish Story	Kelly Bennett	Fiction
Knuffle Bunny: A Cautionary Tale	Mo Willems	Fiction
The Recess Queen	Alexis O'Neill	Fiction
The Hello, Goodbye Window	Norton Juster	Fiction
Rattletrap Car	Phyllis Root	Fiction
Dinosaur Bones	Bob Barner	Nonfiction
Bark, George	Jules Feiffer	Fiction
Stand Tall, Molly Lou Melon	Patty Lovell	Fiction
Into the A, B, Sea	Deborah Lee Rose	Nonfiction

Name _____ Date _____

My Word Wall

Aa	Bb
Cc	**Dd**
Ee	**Ff**
Gg	**Hh**

Name _____ Date _____

My Word Wall

Ii	Jj
Kk	**Ll**
Mm	**Nn**
Oo	**Pp**

Name _____ Date _____

My Word Wall

Qq	**Rr**
Ss	**Tt**
Uu	**Vv**
Ww	**Xx**
Yy	**Zz**

My Writing Ideas

I Am Learning to...

Unpacking Award

You are an unpacking star!!!

You unpacked quickly and quietly during unpacking time!

Packing UP Award

You are a packing-up star!!!

You packed quickly and quietly during packing-up time!

Quiet Bubble Award

____

You are a strong reader!

You used a quiet voice
and stayed inside your quiet bubble
during Reading Workshop time!!!

Resource 5.1

Name ______________________ Date ______________

My Reading Checklist

☐ I used a one-inch voice.

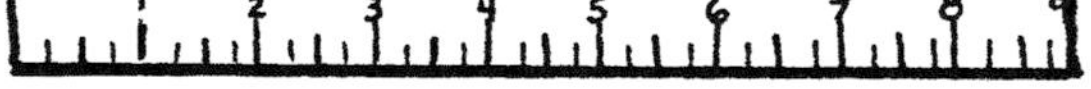

☐ I read in a quiet bubble.

☐ I used my time well.

I read ________ books today.

Resource 5.2 (Kindergarten)

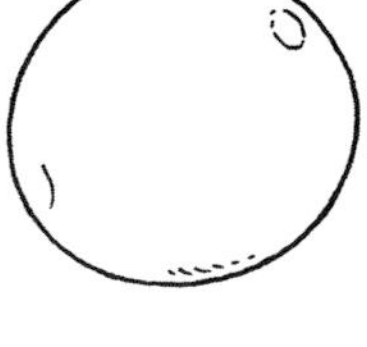

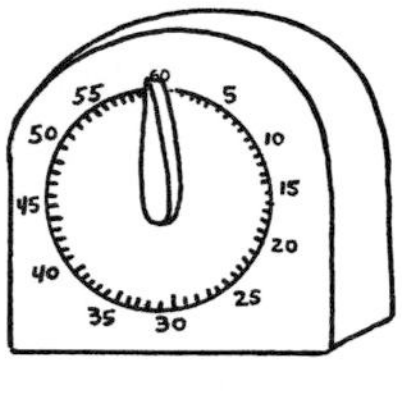

Name _____ Date _____

Reading Workshop Record

| Monday | Tuesday | Wednesday | Thursday | Friday |

Independent Reading

(Title)

(Title)

(Title)

(Title)

(Title)

(Title)

(Title)

(Title)

(Title)

I worked with my teacher.   ☐ Yes   ☐ No

I used a one-inch voice.   ☐ Yes   ☐ No

I used my time well.   ☐ Yes   ☐ No

Name _____ Date _____

My Reading Record

Book Title:

I read from page _____ to page _____

The book genre is:

My comfort level in this book is:
☐ challenging   ☐ just right   ☐ easy

Book Title:

I read from page _____ to page _____

The book genre is:

My comfort level in this book is:
☐ challenging   ☐ just right   ☐ easy

Did you use your reading time well today?   ☐ Yes   ☐ No

Did you meet with your teacher today?   ☐ Yes   ☐ No

Partner 1 _____ Date _____

Partner 2 _____

Partner Reading

	We took turns. 
	We used a one-inch voice. 
	We looked at a book together. 
	We talked about the book. 
	We sat in a quiet bubble. 

Rate your partnership, then circle one task you and your partner want to try harder on tomorrow.

Partner 1 _____ Date _____

Partner 2 _____

Partner Talk

	We treated each other with kindness and respect. 
	We came to partner time prepared to discuss our books. 
	We listened to each other and responded to each other's comments. 
	We made a plan for our next discussion (how many pages we will read). 

One goal we have set for ourselves to improve our conversations is:

_____

_____

_____

Partner Award

_____ and _____
are great partners!

You took turns and were
respectful of each other!

Resource 5.7

Strong Reader Award

_____

You are a strong reader!

You read for _____ minutes during
independent reading time!!!

Resource 5.8

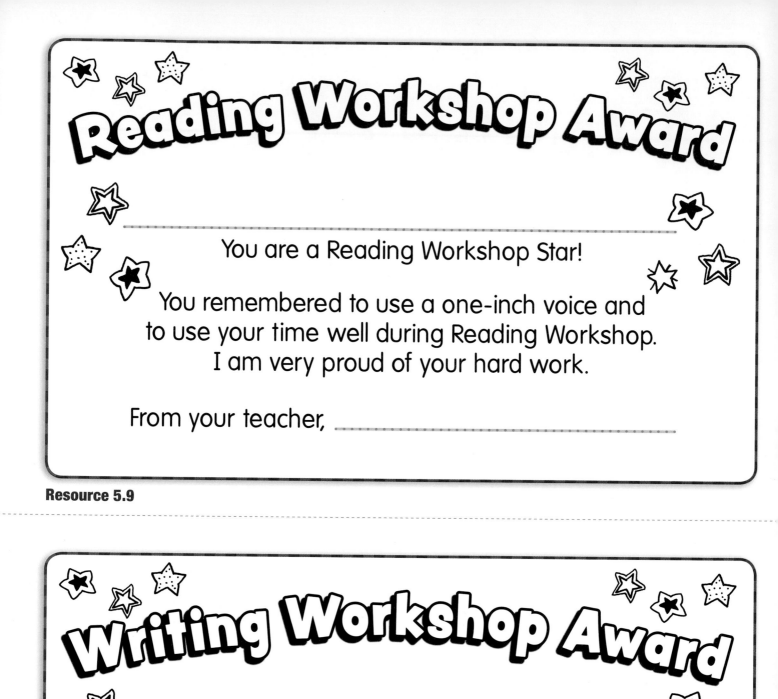

Reading Workshop Award

You are a Reading Workshop Star!

You remembered to use a one-inch voice and
to use your time well during Reading Workshop.
I am very proud of your hard work.

From your teacher, _____

Writing Workshop Award

You are a Writing Workshop Star!

You remembered to use a one-inch voice and
to use your time well during Writing Workshop.
I am very proud of your hard work.

From your teacher, _____

Reading Long and Strong Bookmark

Sit in a quiet bubble.

Read until the time is up.

Take a picture walk first.

Read like we talk.

Will you please be my best friend?

Sure!

Find a favorite part.

Reading Long and Strong Bookmark

Read until the time is up.

Make sure most books are on your level.

Choose an interesting book.

Choose books from different genres.

books

Take a picture walk first.

Find a favorite part.

Small-Group Reading Instruction— Monthly Planning (Sample 1)

Month: _____

Group:	Group:	Group:
Level:	Level:	Level:
Students:	Students:	Students:

Group:	Group:	Group:
Level:	Level:	Level:
Students:	Students:	Students:

Small-Group Reading Instruction—
Monthly Planning (Sample 2)

Month: _____

Group: _____ **Level:** _____
Children:

1. _____ 2. _____
3. _____ 4. _____
5. _____ 6. _____

Teaching Points

_____
_____
_____

Group: _____ **Level:** _____
Children:

1. _____ 2. _____
3. _____ 4. _____
5. _____ 6. _____

Teaching Points

_____
_____
_____

Group: _____ **Level:** _____
Children:

1. _____ 2. _____
3. _____ 4. _____
5. _____ 6. _____

Teaching Points

_____
_____
_____

Group: _____ **Level:** _____
Children:

1. _____ 2. _____
3. _____ 4. _____
5. _____ 6. _____

Teaching Points

_____
_____
_____

Group: _____ **Level:** _____
Children:

1. _____ 2. _____
3. _____ 4. _____
5. _____ 6. _____

Teaching Points

_____
_____
_____

Group: _____ **Level:** _____
Children:

1. _____ 2. _____
3. _____ 4. _____
5. _____ 6. _____

Teaching Points

_____
_____
_____

Small-Group Reading Instruction— Monthly Planning (Complete 4)

Month: _____

Group: _____ **Level:** _____

Students:

1. _____ 2. _____ 3. _____

4. _____ 5. _____ 6. _____

Teaching Points

Process Lessons	Genre Lessons
Strategy Lessons	**Conventions Lessons**

Group: _____ **Level:** _____

Students:

1. _____ 2. _____ 3. _____

4. _____ 5. _____ 6. _____

Teaching Points

Process Lessons	Genre Lessons
Strategy Lessons	**Conventions Lessons**

Small-Group Reading Instruction—
Weekly Planning (Sample 1)

Week of _____

Monday	Tuesday	Wednesday	Thursday	Friday

Week of _____

Monday	Tuesday	Wednesday	Thursday	Friday

Week of _____

Monday	Tuesday	Wednesday	Thursday	Friday

Small-Group Reading Instruction—
Weekly Planning (Sample 2)

Week of _____

	Monday	Tuesday	Wednesday	Thursday	Friday
Group ___	Teaching Point: Text:	Teaching Point: Text:	Teaching Point: Text:	Teaching Point: Text:	Teaching Point: Text:
Group ___	Teaching Point: Text:	Teaching Point: Text:	Teaching Point: Text:	Teaching Point: Text:	Teaching Point: Text:
Group ___	Teaching Point: Text:	Teaching Point: Text:	Teaching Point: Text:	Teaching Point: Text:	Teaching Point: Text:
Group ___	Teaching Point: Text:	Teaching Point: Text:	Teaching Point: Text:	Teaching Point: Text:	Teaching Point: Text:
Group ___	Teaching Point: Text:	Teaching Point: Text:	Teaching Point: Text:	Teaching Point: Text:	Teaching Point: Text:

Small-Group Reading Instruction— Daily Planning (Sample 1)

Level:	Book Title:	Date:

Teaching Points	Students	Notes

Level:	Book Title:	Date:

Teaching Points	Students	Notes

Small-Group Reading Instruction— Daily Planning (Sample 2)

Date: _____

Level:	Book Title:

Teaching Points:	Instructional Notes:

Students	Observations

Next Steps:

Independent Practice to Follow Lesson:	Teaching Points for Next Lesson:

Small-Group Writing Instruction— Monthly Planning (Sample 1)

Month: _____

Group: _____ **Level:** _____

Children:

1. _____ 2. _____

3. _____ 4. _____

5. _____ 6. _____

Teaching Points

_____

_____

_____

Group: _____ **Level:** _____

Children:

1. _____ 2. _____

3. _____ 4. _____

5. _____ 6. _____

Teaching Points

_____

_____

_____

Group: _____ **Level:** _____

Children:

1. _____ 2. _____

3. _____ 4. _____

5. _____ 6. _____

Teaching Points

_____

_____

_____

Group: _____ **Level:** _____

Children:

1. _____ 2. _____

3. _____ 4. _____

5. _____ 6. _____

Teaching Points

_____

_____

_____

Group: _____ **Level:** _____

Children:

1. _____ 2. _____

3. _____ 4. _____

5. _____ 6. _____

Teaching Points

_____

_____

_____

Group: _____ **Level:** _____

Children:

1. _____ 2. _____

3. _____ 4. _____

5. _____ 6. _____

Teaching Points

_____

_____

_____

Small-Group Writing Instruction— Monthly Planning (Complete 4)

Month: _____

Group: _____ **Level:** _____

Students:

1. _____ 2. _____ 3. _____

4. _____ 5. _____ 6. _____

Teaching Points

Process Lessons	**Genre Lessons**
Strategy Lessons	**Conventions Lessons**

Group: _____ **Level:** _____

Students:

1. _____ 2. _____ 3. _____

4. _____ 5. _____ 6. _____

Teaching Points

Process Lessons	**Genre Lessons**
Strategy Lessons	**Conventions Lessons**

Small-Group Writing Instruction—
Weekly Planning (Sample 1)

Week of _____

Monday	Tuesday	Wednesday	Thursday	Friday
Small Groups: Group # _____ Group # _____ And/Or Conferences: 1._____ 2._____ 3._____	Small Groups: Group # _____ Group # _____ And/Or Conferences: 1._____ 2._____ 3._____	Small Groups: Group # _____ Group # _____ And/Or Conferences: 1._____ 2._____ 3._____	Small Groups: Group # _____ Group # _____ And/Or Conferences: 1._____ 2._____ 3._____	Small Groups: Group # _____ Group # _____ And/Or Conferences: 1._____ 2._____ 3._____
Small Groups: Group # _____ Group # _____ And/Or Conferences: 1._____ 2._____ 3._____	Small Groups: Group # _____ Group # _____ And/Or Conferences: 1._____ 2._____ 3._____	Small Groups: Group # _____ Group # _____ And/Or Conferences: 1._____ 2._____ 3._____	Small Groups: Group # _____ Group # _____ And/Or Conferences: 1._____ 2._____ 3._____	Small Groups: Group # _____ Group # _____ And/Or Conferences: 1._____ 2._____ 3._____

Small-Group Writing Instruction—Weekly Planning (Sample 2)

Week of _____

Monday	Tuesday	Wednesday	Thursday	Friday
Teaching Point:	**Teaching Point:**	**Teaching Point:**	**Teaching Point:**	**Teaching Point:**
Students:	**Students:**	**Students:**	**Students:**	**Students:**
Teaching Point:	**Teaching Point:**	**Teaching Point:**	**Teaching Point:**	**Teaching Point:**
Students:	**Students:**	**Students:**	**Students:**	**Students:**

Small-Group Writing Instruction— Daily Planning

Date: _____

Teaching Points:	Teaching Materials:

Students	Observations

Next Steps:

Independent Practice to Follow Lesson:	Teaching Points for Next Lesson:

Reading Toolbox Strategies

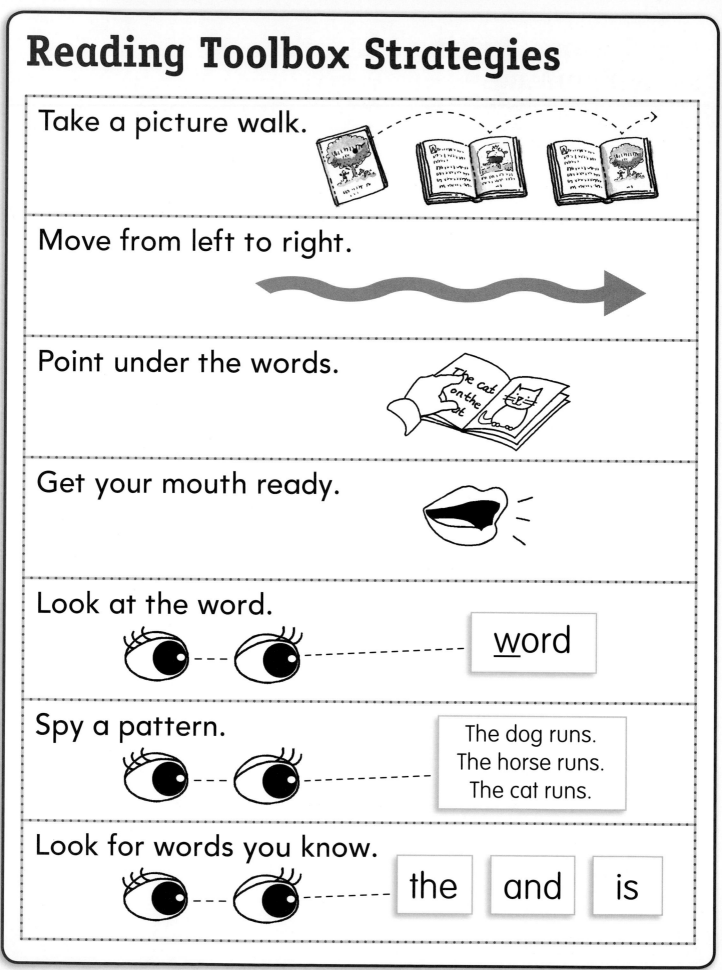

Take a picture walk.

Move from left to right.

Point under the words.

Get your mouth ready.

Look at the word.

word

Spy a pattern.

The dog runs.
The horse runs.
The cat runs.

Look for words you know.

the   and   is

The Great Eight: Management Strategies for the Reading and Writing Classroom © Scholastic Inc. • page 140

Conference Notes

Student: _____ **Date:** _____	**Student:** _____ **Date:** _____	**Student:** _____ **Date:** _____	**Student:** _____ **Date:** _____
Student: _____ **Date:** _____	**Student:** _____ **Date:** _____	**Student:** _____ **Date:** _____	**Student:** _____ **Date:** _____
Student: _____ **Date:** _____	**Student:** _____ **Date:** _____	**Student:** _____ **Date:** _____	**Student:** _____ **Date:** _____
Student: _____ **Date:** _____	**Student:** _____ **Date:** _____	**Student:** _____ **Date:** _____	**Student:** _____ **Date:** _____
Student: _____ **Date:** _____	**Student:** _____ **Date:** _____	**Student:** _____ **Date:** _____	**Student:** _____ **Date:** _____

Post-Conference Notes

Student: _____

Date:	Title of Book/Writing:
Compliment	
Teaching Point	
Future Teaching	

Date:	Title of Book/Writing:
Compliment	
Teaching Point	
Future Teaching	

Date:	Title of Book/Writing:
Compliment	
Teaching Point	
Future Teaching	

Date:	Title of Book/Writing:
Compliment	
Teaching Point	
Future Teaching	

Reading and Writing Conference
Quick Reference

Assess	Observe and gather information (ask questions).
	Formulate compliment and teaching point.

Compliment	Give explicit and authentic compliments (1–2).
	Reinforce behaviors or skills demonstrated.

Teach	Model and explain the ONE thing you will be teaching. Use clear examples.
	• Is it clearly defined? • Is it appropriate for a conference? • Is it a priority?

Try	Observe as the student tries to do what you have taught.
	Coach, if needed, as he/she gains strength.

Clarify	Restate teaching point and connect it to ongoing work.

THE COMPLETE YEAR IN READING AND WRITING

The Great Eight: Management Strategies for the Reading and Writing Classroom is a stand-alone resource—but also part of a K–5 comprehensive reading and writing curriculum, *The Complete Year in Reading and Writing*. Explore any or all of the grade-specific curricular guides inside *The Complete Year*, and you'll find a detailed

curricular calendar that's tied to a developmental continuum and the standards, so you'll know not only what you should be teaching, but also what your students are ready to embrace and what you can reasonably expect of them as successful readers and writers. Additionally, you'll find monthly units of study that integrate reading and writing, with both working together to provide maximum support for your students.

The units are organized around four essential components—process, genre, strategy, and conventions (the Complete 4)—so you're reassured that you're addressing everything your students need to know about reading and writing. What's more, you'll find ready-to-use lessons that offer exemplary teaching and continuous assessment, and a flexible framework that shows you how to structure a year of teaching, a unit, and a lesson—and you can easily adapt all to fit the unique needs and interests of your own students. Each book includes a 17-minute DVD and a four-color gatefold that features a yearlong planner.

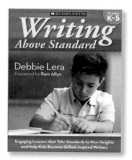

Additionally, Debbie Lera's *Writing Above Standard: Engaging Lessons That Take Standards to New Heights and Help Kids Become Skilled, Inspired Writers* shows you how to use the standards as an inquiry-based guide to excellent writing that enables students to transcend grade-level expectations.

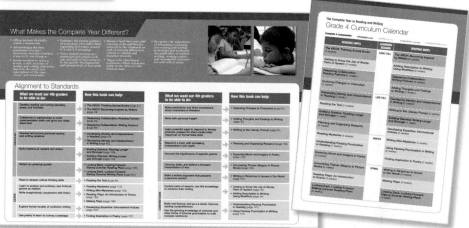